WINNING
MORE
BUSINESS
in
FINANCIAL
SERVICES

How to Score Big with
Referrals and Networking

Michael Salmon

New York   Chicago   San Francisco   Lisbon   London   Madrid   Mexico City
Milan   New Delhi   San Juan   Seoul   Singapore   Sydney   Toronto

1 2 3 4 5 6 7 8 9 10 DOC/DOC 1 8 7 6 5 4 3

ISBN 978-0-07-179184-7
MHID   0-07-179184-1

e-ISBN 978-0-07-179185-4
e-MHID   0-07-179185-X

* * *

To all of the financial services professionals I have had the great pleasure of working with, thank you. Our relationship means more to me than you know. Our success together is the genesis of this book, and I am eternally grateful for the opportunity to help others.

To Harvey Kadden, from the bottom of my heart, thank you. Without you, I would not be where I am today. I love you, man!

Contents

Preface   v

Acknowledgments   vii

Introduction   ix

Chapter 1
Setting Objectives and Preparing Your Strategy   1

Chapter 2
Building Your Network of Essential Partners   23

Chapter 3
Asking for Introductions and Getting What You Want   45

Chapter 4
Prepping to Make a Great Impression   73

Chapter 5
Speaking with Referrals in a Way That Tilts
the Scales in Your Favor   93

Chapter 6
Making Centers of Influence Better Referral Sources   123

Chapter 7
Thriving in Changing Times   145

Chapter 8
Improving Your Efficiency and Effectiveness   167

Chapter 9
Dealing with the What-Ifs   193

Chapter 10
Creating a Referral Network for Life   211

Index   219

Preface

Early in my career, I consistently outsold everyone else on the sales force of a Fortune 500 company. What I was doing was different from what the other 119 salespeople did. I routinely asked my clients and other people I knew for introductions to people they knew, based on specific criteria I used to describe the companies and individuals I wanted to meet. I made it easy for my contacts to introduce me to people who knew the right people, and sometimes to the right people themselves. I closed a lot of business. Over the course of my 30 years in sales, marketing, management, and senior management positions for both publicly traded and privately held companies, I refined this process and demonstrated its value.

When I told my cousin about it and expressed interest in working for his company, Merrill Lynch, he shared my information with his boss. She agreed to meet with me (a perfect example of the *Winning More Business* method in action). She hired me to train Merrill Lynch's advisors, giving me my start in financial services. Today, the company I founded to teach others the *Winning More Business* methodology continues to work with Merrill Lynch all over the country, as well as with financial advisors at major financial institutions, including 50 of the Barron's and Worth's Top 1,000 Financial Advisors and Fortune 500 executives. I have personally worked with the top performers at the bluest of blue chip companies that you read about every day on the front page of the *Wall Street Journal*: Morgan Stanley Smith Barney, UBS,

Wells Fargo Advisors, Sun Trust, Alliance Bernstein, Fiduciary Trust, PIMCO, BlackRock, Lincoln Financial, Bank of America, HSBC, and Credit Suisse, to name a few. I figured out how to access the right people in those organizations and ultimately was able to convince them that my company's programs would lead their people, and in the end their organizations, to spectacular results through the most challenging times this industry has ever seen.

The market crash of 2008 has changed the financial services business forever. People who have money to invest are more cautious and skeptical than ever before, but many are still willing to listen to fresh ideas. Paradoxically, there is more money sitting on the sidelines than ever before, and it's harder for financial services professionals to pick up clients. That's why most wealth management, hedge fund, banking, asset management, and annuity specialists aren't hitting their new acquisition goals. But bringing in new clients is actually as easy as asking—*if you ask the right people in the right way.* In this book, you will learn how to do that.

Acknowledgments

Michael Snell, thank you for your support, prodding, sage advice, friendship, and bringing my concept for a book into reality. If you have a book idea, call Michael.

Libby Koponen, thank you for bringing my ideas to life and pushing me to greater heights, resulting in my best work to date.

Jennifer Ashkenazy and all the people at McGraw-Hill, thank you for believing in me and giving me the opportunity to share this book with many people.

My wife, Holly, thank you for your patience, support, confidence, and putting up with me throughout this process. It did not go unnoticed, and it is greatly appreciated. I love you!

My daughters, Adrie and Alex, thank you for your help when I needed it and for listening to me even when I repeat myself. To my son, Evan, thank you for the talks, support, and encouragement. I love you all!

Lou Lanzillo, my partner in arms, thanks for your support, counsel, wisdom, and friendship.

My parents, Otto and Anne Salmon, thanks for giving me my foundation.

Introduction

SALMON SAYS
"It's not what you know, but whom you know."

An Alliance Bernstein study found that 75 percent of people with investable assets did not know anything about investing their money. Of these people, 80 percent said that they wanted to be introduced to their financial advisors through someone they knew. Equally telling is a survey from *Sales Management* magazine: 90 percent of those surveyed routinely took and returned warm calls. However, only 10 percent took or returned cold calls.

Despite this, fewer than 20 percent of all financial advisors network effectively to get referrals. According to industry experts, the majority of advisors hope for rather than seek referrals. They get their referrals by accident, settling for those that trickle in from clients or friends. Chance introductions like this rarely give advisors the kind of new clients they really want.

Advisors don't ask for referrals because asking makes them uncomfortable. They have never been shown a system like the one in *Winning More Business*, a "how-to" approach to building and leveraging their networks. *Winning More Business* provides a methodical approach for identifying a specific target for a specific reason, figuring out how to build the best links to that target, and then radically speeding up your client acquisition process. You will see how to expand your base of business contacts, leverage your existing relationships, extract promises from your contacts, and track your progress and results. *Winning More Business* is a sustainable, repeatable process that will consistently get you in front of the right people and ensure that those people will hear what you have to say.

There are colleges and degrees for marketing, computer science, accounting, or finance, but not for sales-client development. Selling has been considered something that you either understand instinctively or develop through sales training, or both. There are books that help once you are engaged in the process and speaking to the right person. But if you can't reach the people, you can't use those skills.

Winning More Business shows you how to create a life in which you make only warm calls, regularly reach the right people, and acquire more clients than you ever thought possible. You do this by following a simple process explained and scripted for you every step of the way.

TAKING CONTROL OF YOUR CLIENT ACQUISITION ACTIVITIES—*WINNING THE BUSINESS* STEP BY STEP

Chapter 1: How to create an effective road map by setting clear objectives and developing a supportive, sound strategy.

Chapter 2: How to qualify personal and professional contacts and categorize them appropriately for quick reference.

Chapter 3: How to stage, frame, and deliver your requests to contacts and clients so that you get introductions to exactly the people you want to meet.

Chapter 4: How to prepare for that first call to a referral so that you make a good impression.

Chapter 5: What to say when you make that first call to a referral and in subsequent conversations.

Chapter 6: How to get attorneys and accountants to give you referrals.

Chapter 7: How to thrive in the volatile new normal.

Chapter 8: How to use your time effectively and move people through your pipeline so that most of your new referrals become clients.

Chapter 9: How to handle all the what-ifs that will inevitably arise.

Chapter 10: How to build a network for life.

LET'S GET STARTED

Winning More Business is for everybody. Those who are new to the business will learn a system for building a network of contacts and developing great habits from the beginning of their careers. More experienced advisors will see how to refine their processes to reach their highest potential. For everyone, *Winning More Business* is about working smarter, not harder.

Your new client opportunities are right there for you through introductions made on your behalf by your network of clients and contacts. It will require some work on your part because there are no shortcuts to success; as filmmaker Spike Lee said, "There is no such thing as an overnight success." I guarantee that if you are willing to put in the time and follow what is prescribed in this book, you *will* have the success, prosperity, and book of business that you want.

Keep in mind that you must never look at a client, contact, or referral thinking, "Are you a referral source or prospect, or not?" If you do, people will see through you. You will become the person other people run away from, and you will miss out on some amazing relationships, too. Some of the people you meet through this process may never become clients, but they may become friends or sources of referrals. And that is fine. Everyone needs more good relationships, especially financial advisors. You never know when you are going to have that "golden moment," the meeting or instant that catapults your practice to a whole new level. This book is going to give you the tools to create those moments, take advantage of opportunities when they arise, and create an ongoing referral-generating machine for yourself.

The advisors I coach have incorporated these time-tested ideas into their daily routines and achieved great results with them. I tell my clients what they need to know, not what they want to hear. What I tell them is what I tell you in this book. It has served my clients well over time, and if you are open to the ideas and do what the book recommends, it will serve you well too.

Note: The names of individuals and locations used as examples throughout the book were changed to preserve clients' anonymity. The stories and examples come from years of experience in the business, focusing on how to get what so many people want but can't consistently find: referrals that lead to new clients.

1

Setting Objectives and Preparing Your Strategy

Kevin was like many other financial advisors: he wanted more clients, but he had no plan for finding them. He did ask his clients and friends to let him know if they met or knew people who might need his services, but this vague request generally led nowhere. As I said, "If you continue to network this way, you are simply spinning your wheels. People can't help you unless you tell them exactly what you want to accomplish and what kind of person you want to meet."

Many of your peers may think they know how to get referrals because they have sporadically used their networks to get names and introductions. They may not admit it, but generally the people they meet this way aren't the kind of people they want and need to be meeting. Their random approach to referrals means that they spend a great deal of time pursuing people who are highly unlikely to become clients. Yes, they "know a lot of people" or have a list of contacts. But that's all they have because most of the time, they just wing it. They have no plan.

This chapter shows you the importance of having a road map—a clear path that can keep you focused on networking activities that get the best results possible—and teaches you how to create one. You'll learn how to set an objective for what you want to accomplish, develop a supporting strategy, and incorporate an accountability and responsibility mechanism that will keep you focused. These are the essential steps in getting the outcomes you desire.

If you do everything prescribed in this chapter, you will be well on your way to getting where you want to be: receiving better and more qualified introductions, scheduling more appointments, and closing more business in far less time than you ever imagined.

John Wooden, the most successful coach in college basketball history, had a simple objective for every game: to win. His record includes a .804 winning percentage over a 23-year period and 10 NCAA championships, including 7 in a row from 1966 to 1973 at UCLA. He said, "Failing to prepare is preparing to fail." He may have lost a few games, but he was always prepared—and he usually won. If you have a solid objective and a sound supporting strategy that you follow consistently, you'll make it easy for people to open doors for you. You'll become very busy working only on warm calls. It all starts with a plan!

SETTING AN OBJECTIVE

Start by thinking about your current book of business and what you want to accomplish going forward in a careful, methodical way. There are no shortcuts. Acting randomly and impulsively won't work in today's economy, even if it has worked for you in the past.

Kevin is a good example. He'd been in the business for 20 years, and he was used to always being at the top. He prided himself on being a people person who could communicate with anyone, think on his feet ("wing it"), and get the results he needed. As he said, "Once I get in front of a new prospect, I'm dangerous. I will close them."

Unfortunately, he was not meeting a lot of new prospective clients that met his profile. He knew he needed to do things differently because "winging it" was just not working anymore. Here is how he started and how you should start, too.

Have a Clear Mental Image of Your Ideal Clients

When I asked Kevin about his ideal clients, he told me that they were entertainers, professional athletes, and the managers and accountants who work with them. He was able to articulate his target clearly to his network of contacts—there was no ambiguity or mystery about whom Kevin wanted to meet. Can you describe the people you'd like to meet that clearly? If you're using any of the following phrases to describe your targets, your description is too vague:

- *"High-net-worth people."* Your definition of a high-net-worth person and your contacts' definition could vary.

Your contacts may be thinking $5 million in liquid assets, while you may be thinking $1 million or $3 million. The point is that since your definitions are different, asking to be introduced to a "high-net-worth person" will create confusion, not clarity.

- *"Wealthy people" or "successful people."* Again, people define these words very differently. To you, "successful" may mean someone with millions to invest, but to one of your contacts, "successful" may mean someone who loves and enjoys her work. Again, the definitions vary too much to be useful.

- *"People like you."* What does that mean? Should the person be 55 years old, married, with three children, and the owner of a business? This vague description is also too subjective to give to anyone in your network and expect a perfect match.

- *"People who don't have the time to manage their own money and could benefit from a smart advisor."* In theory, this is a good idea and description, but when have you ever heard anyone say, "I'm looking for a financial advisor because I don't have time to manage my own money"?

The more clearly you can describe the kind of people you want to meet, the easier it is for people to think of other people they know who fit the description. By visualizing the kind of people you want to meet, defining them clearly to yourself, and then describing that profile vividly to others, you help the people in your network make introductions for you.

Here are some phrases from successful advisors to get you started on creating a clear mental picture of the people you want to meet:

- Wealth creators the second or third time around—those who have sold a few businesses. Also referred to as "serial entrepreneurs"
- Entrepreneurs
- Business owners
- Family offices (working with the patriarch, matriarch, children, and relatives—generally multigenerational)
- People who have sold their businesses
- Professional athletes
- Senior managers of publicly traded companies
- Corporate executives
- Retirees (from publicly traded and/or privately held companies)
- Retirees from management positions
- Divorcées
- Widows
- Doctors
- Dentists
- CPAs
- Attorneys
- People who have inherited wealth
- Nonprofits
- Institutions

As you went through this list, did you start thinking about people you knew that fit some of the descriptions? Chances are that your clients and contacts will, too. These words provide clear visual cues; when they hear them, your contacts will start thinking about people they know that fit the image.

Another easy way to come up with descriptive phrases is to imagine that you and I were at a party and I asked, "What kind of people do you work with?" What would you say in response to that?

Make Your Objective Narrowly Focused, Quantifiable, and Measurable

Think about how many new clients and the dollar amount of net new assets you want and in what time period. Kevin was going through a divorce and was highly motivated to double his income as soon as possible. We agreed that his objective was to bring in $75 million in net new assets (15 new clients at an average of $5 million each) over an 18-month period. In order to come up with your numbers, think about what *you* want to accomplish over what period of time, and then do the arithmetic.

Put Your Objective Together

Now that you know exactly the type of people you want to meet through a warm introduction (being introduced through a connection) and how many new clients and net new assets you need over what period of time, you are ready to create your road map.

Make your objective well thought out, clearly defined, and narrow enough to achieve the desired result. Here are some examples:

- Kevin's objective: Bring in $75 million in net new assets in the next 18 months by utilizing and leveraging my professional and personal contacts to work with more entertainers, professional athletes, and the managers, accountants, and attorneys who work with professional athletes and entertainers.

- *Example objective for a two-person team with more than 20 years in the business that works with businesspeople:* Bring in $50 million in new assets in the next 12 months by leveraging our personal and professional network of contacts to work with more serial entrepreneurs, corporate executives, and retired corporate executives.

- *Example objective of a sole practitioner with 5 years in the business who works with professionals:* Bring in $15 million in net new assets over the next 12 months by leveraging my personal and professional network of contacts to work with more doctors and dentists and their practices in the Atlanta area.

- *Example objective of a team with 10 years in the business that works with "money in motion":* Bring in $25 million in net new assets over the next 12 months by leveraging our personal and professional network of contacts to work with more widows, divorcées, people who have or are about to have a liquidity event, and people who are about to sell or have recently sold a business.

As you saw, the objectives that these advisors created were clear, definite, specific, and complete. Using these examples as guidelines, write your objective here. Begin with how much in net assets you want to bring in over what time frame, and be as specific and complete as possible about the kind of people you want to meet.

Create Your Objective

_____

_____

_____

_____

DEVELOPING A SUPPORTING STRATEGY

Now that you know what you want to accomplish and have written it down succinctly, it is time to work on creating an effective road map. This is your supporting strategy to keep you focused, make it easy for people to help you, and get the outcome you desire.

There are four steps involved in planning your strategy; they follow a sequential order:

1. Think about ways to achieve your objective.
2. Determine which ideas make the most sense.
3. Put together the action plan with timelines.
4. Execute the plan.

Think About Ways to Achieve Your Objective

Go ahead and put down any networking ideas that come to mind. You may have tried some of them already, and there may be some that you'd like to try—both are fine. There is no such thing as a bad idea. So just start listing whatever you think might get you where you want to go. Push yourself. Think outside the box and list every idea that pops into your mind. For example, Kevin's objective was to bring in $75 million in net new assets by utilizing his network of contacts to gain access to and work with more entertainers, professional athletes, and the managers, attorneys, and accountants who work with them. Kevin came up with these ideas to achieve his objective:

- Name 50 individuals (entertainers and athletes) that I would like to have as clients and ask my athlete and entertainer clients if they know these people; if they do, ask for a warm introduction on my behalf.
- Ask clients who are entertainers for introductions to or contact information for two or three entertainers they know who are not on my list of 50.
- Ask clients who are professional athletes for introductions to or contact information for two or three professional athletes they know who are not on my list of 50.
- Identify my advocate clients—those people who really believe in me. Ask them for introductions, naming names when I have them.
- Ask business managers I work with for introductions to or contact information for two or three of their clients.
- Ask clients' accountants for introductions to or contact information for two or three of their clients.
- Ask my contacts for introductions to or contact information for two or three people who meet my client profile.
- Go through my client attorney list and reach out to them for introductions to people that meet my profile and/or two or three other attorneys in their firm that they'd be comfortable introducing me to.

- Identify partners in law firms that specialize in the areas I am targeting and get my center of influence (COI) contacts to introduce me to individuals who meet my profile.
- Hold strategic topical events for clients and have them invite people they know who meet my profile.
- Sponsor events.
- Get active in associations and be visible.

Now that you have seen how Kevin planned to meet his objective, you can start thinking about ways to meet yours. Start your list here:

Determine Which Ideas Make the Most Sense

Now take a look at your list and decide what it's realistic to do on a consistent basis. For example, when Kevin read his list over, he realized that he'd never be able to do all 12 activities. As he reflected on his ideas, he also realized that some were really good and some were too time-consuming or too unrealistic, or had other problems.

You have to streamline your plan. Do not take on more than you can handle, or you'll always feel guilty for not doing everything you are supposed be doing, and that's not a good feeling.

Kevin came up with six things that he could do consistently. Here they are, with his reasoning in italics:

- Identify 50 entertainers and 50 professional athletes that I want to meet through a warm introduction and ask my clients for introductions. *Kevin knew that his high-profile professional athlete and entertainment clients could get him access to almost anyone he would put on a list. Also, he knew them well, and he felt that asking for a specific introduction to someone by name would work better than a broad request for "an entertainer or athlete."*
- Ask business managers I work with for introductions to or contact information for two or three of their clients. *Kevin had relationships with three business managers that were strong enough for him to feel comfortable asking for warm introductions. He estimated that if he got nine warm introductions, he would close three of them.*
- Ask the accountants of clients for introductions to or contact information for two or three clients. *Kevin had*

strong relationships with four accountants specializing in athletes and entertainers. He thought he could get at least eight warm introductions through the accountants and close three of them over the next 18 months.

- Identify partners in law firms that specialize in the areas I am targeting and access these individuals through a warm introduction from my client and center of influence (COI) contacts. *Kevin felt that all 75 of his clients would be comfortable giving him the contact information for their attorney. And if he already had the attorney's name, he could call her directly (please see Chapter 6 for scripting on calling COIs). In addition, Kevin thought that his accountant and business manager contacts would also make introductions on his behalf.*

- Ask people in my personal network for introductions to or contact information for two or three people they know that meet my client profile. *Kevin estimated that he had more than 350 people in his personal network, and he felt that many of them would be open to making a warm introduction on his behalf, which would lead to getting the names of at least 40 prospective clients through a warm introduction.*

- Hold strategic topical events for clients and have them invite people they know who meet my profile. *Kevin felt that he could get at least 10 of his professional football clients to invite at least 4 of their teammates to a dinner either prior to minicamp, just before training camp in July, or during an off week. That would equate to accessing at least 40 prospective clients through a warm introduction.*

Do you worry that six isn't enough? Remember Red Auerbach, the architect for the great Boston Celtics championship teams? A writer once asked him why, since the game was always changing, he ran only six plays. Red shouted, "You see those banners hanging up in the rafters? Those are championship banners. We'll continue to run six plays until we stop putting up banners!"

INCORPORATING ACCOUNTABILITY
INTO YOUR PLAN WITH TIMELINES

It's one thing to come up with a clear mental picture of exactly the kind of people you want to meet and great ways to do that. Next comes the hard part—actually doing it. Make this easier by figuring out what you can do when and committing to specific dates. Kevin created the timelines in Tables 1-1 to 1-4.

Table 1-1 Timeline for Lists of Entertainers and Athletes I Want as Clients

Action Item	Targeted Date	Date Completed
Complete prep list of top 50 entertainers and pro athletes I want as clients	July 17	July 17
Start calling clients for introductions	July 24	Ongoing
Start calling referrals and getting meetings	July 31	Ongoing

Table 1-2   Timeline for Lists of Business Managers, Accountants, and Attorneys

Action Item	Targeted Date	Date Completed
Complete prep list of business managers, accountants, and attorneys I want to contact	August 1	July 31
Start calling COIs for introductions	August 3	Ongoing
Start calling referrals and getting meetings	August 10	Ongoing

Table 1-3   Timeline for List of People in My Personal Network

Action Item	Targeted Date	Date Completed
Complete prep list of people in my personal network I will contact and ask for a warm introduction	July 24	July 23
Start calling contacts for introductions	July 26	Ongoing
Start calling referrals and getting meetings	August 1	Ongoing

Table 1-4   Timeline for Staging Events

Action Item	Targeted Date	Date Completed
Complete prep list of top 20 pro athlete clients I want to ask for help in staging an event	June 4	June 5
Call to get a commitment from 10 to stage the event	June 6	June 10
Schedule the 10 events	Ongoing	Ongoing

Here's how to fill in each field:

- *Action items.* Succinctly detail what needs to be done. Kevin included some of his strategy points. You should list all of them.
- *Targeted date.* Include target dates for when you plan to do what. Having a specific goal like this and holding yourself accountable to it will keep you focused, help you drive the process, and keep things moving.
- *Date completed.* When you actually do something, write down the date. This is a check and balance that will show how you are doing and whether you are keeping your commitments. Sometimes these dates will get pushed out because of circumstances beyond your control—that is okay, as long as these times are exceptions and do not become the rule. If you find that you are consistently missing your deadlines, do not get despondent or frustrated. This is new for you. Just redo your action plan with more realistic timelines.

PUTTING QUANTIFIABLE METRICS INTO YOUR PLAN

If you cannot measure it, you cannot manage it.
—Paul Kazarian, Investment Management Professional

The *referral network sustainable process* works because it blends the objective and the strategy with numbers-based accountability and responsibility metrics. This gives you set standards for tracking your progress and measuring results. When you achieve these specific numbers-based standards every week and every month, you *will* see immediate results.

What separates the players from the fakers is behavior change. The best of the best talk the talk, but, more important, they walk the walk. Are you motivated to stick to the plan you have made?

Progress Report with Measurable Standards of Performance

Accountability and responsibility guarantee a consistent, robust pipeline of activity. They help you develop more and better-qualified leads. Ed Koch, former mayor of New York, used to go around the city saying, "How am I doing?" and recording the answers he got.

Your metrics, like his, show you exactly how you are doing. The standards of performance and critical success factors that follow are based on time-tested results—use them as a guideline when creating your own. They will give you a return on investment (ROI), your payoff from all your hard work. You've heard before that sales is a numbers game. There is a lot of truth to that. Start thinking realistically about how often you will commit to the following critical success factors:

- *Number of asks per week or per month.* It all starts with making your planned initial client or contact calls on a weekly basis. In Chapter 3, you will be given scripts to show you how to ask so that you get the outcome you want. Now, you just need to decide how many times per week or per month you will ask clients for introductions.

  To help you think about this number, I have found that the average advisor commits to making 4 asks per week, or 16 per month. The numbers vary based on the time you devote to business development and the number of new clients you want to bring in.

- *Number of referral names received per month.* You will have enough people in your client and contact list to make many warm calls and get you closer to the person you want to meet through a warm introduction. Realistically, how many names do you think you will receive from those asks on a monthly basis? Track this field monthly, not weekly, so that you don't get discouraged by the ups and downs that can take place on a weekly basis. Monthly is a better representation of consistent activity. Again, the numbers will vary based on your ability to follow the scripts in Chapter 3 and articulate exactly the type of person you want to meet. It is my experience that advisors who stick to the plan and follow the scripts receive referral names at least 60 percent of the time.

- *Number of referral meetings scheduled per month.* Kevin believed that once he met people, he could close them—as he said, "I just need more at bats."

    This is where you get into the batter's box of the game of opportunity. If you are scheduling meetings, you are getting closer to your goal of bringing in new clients and net new assets. If you make the referral calls as described in Chapter 5, you will be well positioned to get meetings. Experience has shown me that at least 60 percent of your referrals will agree to meet with you.

- *Number of second referral meetings scheduled per month.* The actual number of second meetings with referrals will depend on how the first meetings went. Many variables influence that; for example: Is this referral a good fit? Did you get along? What was the timing? Does the referral need an advisor? Chapter 5 gives detailed plans and scripts for having effective second meetings with referrals. Of the referrals that Kevin met, 75 percent took second meetings with him. Many advisors tell me that 50 percent of referrals who agreed to a first meeting agree to a second. You know your business—once you are face-to-face with people, how many take a second meeting with you?

- *Number of new clients per month, per quarter, or per year.* How many of those referrals with whom you met a second time do you think will become clients? Kevin had a 75 percent close ratio with them, and this is pretty typical. Track your progress. Whether you record numbers in this field by month, by quarter, or annually depends on your book of business, the kind of people you target, and how you want to measure yourself. The important thing is to enter the numbers.

Table 1-5 shows how Kevin's numbers looked the first month.

Table 1-5   Kevin's Numbers for the First Month

Kevin	
Number of Touches per Week or per Month	4/16
Number of New Referral Names to Contact per Month	8
Number of Meetings Scheduled with Referrals per Month	4
Number of Second Meetings with These Referrals per Month	2
Number of New Clients per Month	1

EXECUTING YOUR PLAN

The final step is actually executing your plan and keeping careful track of the results. Doing this well requires discipline and work, but it will improve your chances of achieving overwhelming success.

Consider a bank's wealth management team whose six top advisors completed the process you just reviewed and worked on a six-month coaching program with me. The regional vice president, Jeff, wanted his group to exceed its current monthly net new asset goals via networking over the next 12 months. We agreed to track the data monthly but to do the real evaluation quarterly.

When we went over the numbers at the end of the first quarter, people had made fewer networking calls than we had projected. However, the number of new contacts was close to what we had projected, and the number of actual first and second meetings was between acceptable and exceptional. The actual number of new clients and net new assets in dollars exceeded the forecast we had made for the quarter.

After a few jokes and kudos all around, I asked the group members what these numbers told them. They said that once they got an opportunity, their "hit ratio" was outstanding. They also realized that if they increased the number of initial calls they made, they could have even greater success, create more revenue for the bank, generate more opportunities for themselves and others, and put more money in their pockets.

They left the room committed to doing even better the next quarter—and they did. In the second quarter, they found more new clients and their net new assets increased by 40 percent. What was fascinating to me was watching the members of the group review their activities in black and white. Their confidence level rose with the numbers. By clearly defining their goals, formalizing their process, and tracking their progress, they held themselves accountable and achieved their highest-ever performance levels.

Kevin stuck to his plan, and the results were immediate for him, too. In the first 11 months of sticking to his new referral-networking process, Kevin exceeded his own expectations and was so busy with prospect meetings, making presentations, and having numerous follow-up meetings that he didn't need to make cold calls anymore.

Maybe you think all this sounds too good to be true, or maybe you have decided to call people you know to get more and better-qualified leads. But whatever you think, whether you are an expert or a novice at networking, an introvert or an extrovert, you need to have a plan that gives you a sustainable process, focus, purpose, strategy, and tactics.

Have you actually completed your networking objective and strategy? If you haven't, reread the parts of this chapter that you skipped and complete the forms. Remember, you are building your networking referral process link by link. In order to have a solid foundation, you must follow the directions. Just stay focused on the process and consistently exceed your weekly, monthly, and quarterly goals, and great things will happen for you, just as they did for Kevin and for those six advisors.

Chapter 1 Summary Form

Objective:

_____

_____

_____

Strategy:

_____

_____

_____

_____

Action items with timelines:

_____

_____

_____

_____

_____

_____

_____

_____

Accountability metrics:

_____

_____

_____

_____

_____

2

Building Your Network
of Essential Partners

SALMON SAYS

"Peel the onion. Sometimes you have to get through many layers until you get to the core, the right person."

Ron, a very successful advisor in southern California, works predominantly with serial entrepreneurs—people who have sold a business more than once. He's an avid golfer and a member of an exclusive club in Orange County. Ron uses golf as part of his business development and client management strategy. We worked on putting together his A, B, C, and D lists of contacts whom he wanted to ask for "warm introductions." He is also a watch lover who had bought many expensive watches from his jeweler, Benny, whom he knew to be an avid golfer and who was solidly entrenched on his D list. I proposed Benny as a source of referrals, but Ron was skeptical.

"Benny's friends aren't investors!"

"You have a friendly relationship with him—maybe he has similar relationships with exactly the kind of people you want to meet," I said.

So Ron agreed to try it. He told Benny that he wanted to meet people who had sold their businesses and asked if he would be comfortable introducing him to them. Ron suggested golf and a dinner at his club so that he could explain a little more about his line of work. Over the course of 18 holes and dinner, Ron familiarized Benny with his business and his goals. Shortly thereafter, Benny made several introductions that resulted in Ron's picking up two big clients.

To achieve results like Ron's, you need to think about your network the right way. Everyone has a network. It doesn't matter whether you have contact information stored in your head or on LinkedIn or Facebook, or whether you put people's names and information in your Rolodex, PDA, or address book—somewhere, you have lists of the people you know. Whatever the length or form of your list, you need to categorize and prioritize it. Then and only then can you effectively ask your contacts to help you gain access to more of the people you want to meet. Building your network is like growing your bank account: you will get out of it what you put into it.

DETERMINE THE PEOPLE WHO SHOULD BE ON YOUR LIST

Start by creating a list of your contacts. As you do this, think in broader terms than just clients. Consider *all* the people in your life: remember, Ron's referral source was his jeweler.

I am sure there are people in your life who can open a door for you, too. But you need to figure out who they are before you can ask for their help. These are some of the people who should be on your list:

- *Current clients.* Over time, you have established a good rapport with each of these people. You should feel comfortable calling any of them and feel confident that they would give you a positive response.
- *Former clients.* Sometimes you still have a strong relationship with these people, and they still hold you in high regard. If that is the case, they are potential sources of referrals, even though you're no longer working together. In fact, some of them may be more helpful than your current clients.
- *Prospective clients.* Sometimes people who never become clients are the best referral sources. They may not meet your criteria, or for whatever reason you may not meet theirs, but you like them, they like you, and a friendship or strong relationship has evolved. Do not overlook these people; they may know people that you want to know and be willing to make the introductions.
- *CPAs and attorneys.* You've probably been told often that these people can be your best referral sources—in fact, they are such potential gold mines that Chapter 6 is devoted to how to get them on your side. Any CPAs and attorneys you know should be on your list.
- *Essential partners.* These are people you know because their organization has provided service to you and your firm: suppliers, wholesalers, or consultants. If you have developed a strong association with any of these people,

put them on your list. They know your firm, and they know what you do at work. It's worth putting them on your list and finding out whom they know.

- *Family.* Family members generally go out of their way for one another, simply because they are family. Don't just think of immediate family. Think of your extended family—your brother-in-law's sister, distant cousins, and so on.

- *Close friends.* These are people you can always count on, because they have your best interests at heart. Always include them on your list.

- *People you know casually.* These are people you don't know well—you see them socially, or at your golf or tennis club, or at your child's school or sporting events. You respect each other and may have similar interests. If you have a good feeling about each other, these people belong on your list, too. You'd be surprised at how many people like this you know and how many of them can introduce you to the people you want to meet if you approach them in the right way.

- *Professional contacts.* Think about people with whom you have a purely professional relationship: your haircutter, doctor, physical therapist, or jeweler.

- *Alumni.* These are people from your past, either from work or from school. Carl, an advisor, was telling me that he went to a 20-year college reunion fishing trip for a weekend with 20 other guys. Carl rekindled many relationships and developed additional opportunities after letting people know about the kind of people he worked with. Once you reach out to these people, it is likely that they can be as helpful to you as they were to Carl. Do not underestimate the likelihood of these people opening up a door for you, either. However, you need to pick your spots carefully. Carl told me that he would not have had those types of conversations at his high school or college reunion, as anyone who tried to talk about business in this way would get a very cold reception.

You may think that some of the people who came to mind as you were looking over these categories would not be good referral sources because you think they don't know the kind of people you want to meet. That is the wrong way to think. Suppose you know a facilities director casually and you want to meet business owners. You dismissed the facilities director because you thought the people he knew would not be people you want as clients. By thinking that way, you may well completely miss a great opportunity; what if the facilities director really likes you and has a brother-in-law who owns a large, successful business?

At first, Ron thought of his jeweler the way some people might think of that facilities director. Once he changed his thinking and regarded the jeweler as someone who could introduce him to the kinds of people he wanted to meet, he got a couple of great new clients. You need to think more openly about the people you know, too.

CATEGORIZE THE PEOPLE ON YOUR LIST AS As, Bs, Cs, AND Ds

The kinds of conversations you will have with people on your lists will vary, because you have different relationships with different people. The way you speak, what you say, and the details you share will depend upon how well you know each person. What you tell your brother will be different from what you tell a wholesaler. What these people are willing to do for you will vary, too.

That's why you need to categorize your contact list appropriately into four levels. Categorizing your contacts makes your list easier to use and more effective. Your list may be hundreds of names long—once you've categorized everyone, you can look for your target among your powerful allies first, rather than searching through hundreds of names.

Your A List: Advocates

These people are your *champions*! They have the highest regard for you, and they can be counted on to sing your praises and brag about you. They also have the influence to command respect from others. You can contact your advocates at almost any time for advice, connections, referrals, or just about anything else. An advocate will sometimes offer help without being asked, because true advocates are constantly thinking about ways to promote you. They want you to be successful and often volunteer to help in any way they can. When opportunity presents itself, their passionate belief in you comes through loud and clear.

Chris, an advisor down South, had such an advocate in Freddie, his barber. When Chris told Freddie that he wanted to meet more business owners through "warm introductions," Freddie practically cut him off with, "Come down on

Saturday morning, and I will introduce you to a few of my clients I know you would want to meet."

Chris showed up as planned, doughnuts in hand, and met two business owners. One of them, Mike, was in the process of selling his company. Chris and Mike had a great conversation that led to several follow-up meetings at which they talked about Chris's experience handling liquidity events. Within four months, Mike's business was finally sold, and Chris became Mike's financial advisor; he is currently managing $20 million of Mike's assets. Without the introduction from Freddie the barber, it is highly doubtful that Chris and Mike would ever have met. Your advocates will do the same sort of thing for you. They want to help; all you have to do is let them know how they can.

Your B List: Brethren/Buddies

These people are like advocates, but they are not as vocal, and they are more low-key about their love and praise for you. They're family members, close friends, and other people you know well. You can have candid conversations with your buddies; they are people that you rely on and trust. They know you and will make themselves available to you because of your friendship. They love you unconditionally, win, lose, or draw, and they are there for you when you need them most. That's what friends and family do for each other.

Years ago, when I was starting my business, I told my cousin Harvey about my business model and my interest in doing work for his former company, Merrill Lynch. He shared my information with his boss—without that intro-duction, I would not have my platform in financial services and you would not be reading this book. It all started with one focused conversation with my cousin—a buddy. You probably have buddies, too, who will be there for you.

Your C List: Casual Contacts

These are people you are friendly with, but do not know well. Maybe they're friends of friends, people you know profes-sionally, previous clients, prospects, vendors, or alumni. Con-sider how many people they know—maybe some of them can help you, as Rachel was helped by one of her C contacts.

Rachel, an advisor, wanted to get more traction with doctors in a particular oncology practice. Rachel had Meg, an annuity wholesaler, sponsor events at the office. Rachel was a little reluctant to ask Meg for help because they were not friends but professional acquaintances. I asked Rachel: "Do you like Meg? Is Meg a good person? Is she good at what she does? Is she thought highly of by doctors you know?" Rachel said yes to all of these questions. Lastly, I asked, "If roles were reversed and Meg asked if *you* had an in at another office, would you help her open it?"

Rachel said she would—and that changed her perspective on Meg and made her feel more comfortable asking Meg for help. Meg did make the call on Rachel's behalf, and since then they have become friends, shared additional business relationships, and opened doors for each other. Both of their practices have grown as a result.

Your D List: Diamonds in the Rough

This list consists of people that you wouldn't think could actually help you, but who may well know more of the right people than you think they do. How many people does your physical therapist, dry cleaner, or personal trainer see in a week? They probably know of many people who can help you.

Remember Ron, the advisor who asked his jeweler for help. If you think Ron should look elsewhere for introductions, think again! That is the wrong way to think. Everyone who knows this jeweler loves him, so the jeweler has great relationships with all of his clients. If anyone ever called Ron using the jeweler's name, Ron would pay attention out of respect for the relationship he has with the jeweler. That's how this works. People we don't often think of as links can be unexpected and invaluable resources. It's all about the strength of their relationships. The person you see as just a jeweler has taken his relationships and built them into his network. In addition, he has an incredibly successful business. If you can tap into this network through him, that increases the size and power of your own network. That's the way you should be thinking.

However, not every diamond in the rough is an appropriate person to ask for an introduction to a referral. Before you ask a D contact for a warm introduction, ask yourself the following questions:

- What is the strength of the relationship you have with this person?
- How do *you* feel about this person?

- How is this person perceived by others?
- Is this person respected?
- Do other people value this person's opinion?

If you feel good about the answers, then someone like Ron's jeweler would be a good person for you to add to your D list.

INCORPORATE SOCIAL MEDIA INTO THE MIX

Social media should be viewed as a complement to traditional in-person networking and as such can be an important tool. People use social media to:

- Make connections
- Use and create content
- Seek or share an opinion

Online social networking represents an opportunity to leverage the people who are on your A, B, C, and D lists. However, before you embark on any social media endeavor, check with your organization's compliance department—it may have rules against doing so.

If it doesn't, the three most popular avenues for online networking are:

- LinkedIn—strictly professional (think business after-hours party)
- Facebook—predominantly social (think reunion party)

- Twitter—mainly business, but can be social, too (think speed dating)

Here are some of the things you can do on each that will help you distinguish yourself and put you in a position to get the most out of your social media activities.

LinkedIn

LinkedIn was created specifically to help businesspeople network professionally. It is an excellent online tool that allows professionals at companies of all sizes and kinds to congregate, network, expand professional alliances, and maintain a contact list. But unlike an ordinary list of people you know and trust in business, your LinkedIn list contains details (such as work history and the person's other contacts) and keeps itself up-to-date.

LinkedIn is all about connections. Once someone you know has joined your network, or you have joined his, you get to see all the people he knows, what those people do, and where they work.

Connections on LinkedIn are by invitation only, so start by carefully selecting people to add to your network: clients, people you've done business with before, people you know through others, former colleagues, and so on. You can invite anyone to become a connection. Once you have added a few connections to your network, LinkedIn suggests other people that you may know; contacting these people will, of course, help you expand your network. Your connections can be used to build up your direct connections (people you know), your connections to their connections (termed *second-degree connections*), and even the connections of your second-degree connections. All of these can be used to gain introductions.

One good way to get this going is ask your clients to connect with you. Once you've established a connection, look at that person's connections. Is there someone your client is connected to whom you'd like to meet? If so, make a list of those clients and potential referrals, and once you've read Chapter 3, talk to your clients about making the introduction.

I do not recommend letting the technology do that for you. Use technology to help identify the people you'd like to meet. Then, even if your client suggests sending the person an e-mail introducing yourself, make the phone call. It is too easy for people to either not respond to an e-mail or respond by saying they're not interested. Also, unless your client says something, the referral doesn't know how strong your relationship with your client is and may be skeptical. Thus, I recommend speaking to your contact or client in person and asking her to make the introduction, or getting the phone number of the person you want to meet and calling. A conversation works much better than e-mail does.

Proper Protocol on LinkedIn

This business-oriented, after-hours social network can open doors for you if you follow the proper protocol:

- *Be professional.* This is a serious social network, and first impressions are lasting. Since all communication takes place online, people will form an opinion based on what they read. Set the right tone. Think résumé.

- *Be honest, accurate, and forthcoming.* Your credibility is on the line here. Do not exaggerate or inflate *anything*! One bad word is more powerful than 10 recommendations.

- *Be persuasive.* Sell yourself and get people excited about you. Pretend that you are at a business after-hours function and realize that there is a potential business connection. Be engaging, but don't go overboard. Give people a compelling reason that piques their curiosity. Think about what distinguishes you from other advisors or what your clients say about you. It could be your years of experience, your expertise working with Fortune 500 executives, your client retention rate, or something else.

- *Be direct.* Fellow LinkedIn members have an appreciation for candor—they don't want to read fluff. This is a business social networking tool, and in business, time is of the essence. Make your point.

- *Be focused.* Do not try to be all things to all people. The more focused you are, the closer you will get to the people you want to be connected to.

- *Be involved.* Join groups. Groups are an excellent way to meet people online and build your network. There are hundreds of them out there. Pick the ones that resonate with you.

- *Be active.* Check out the "people you know" box on your LinkedIn home page. LinkedIn mines the web of people created by your contacts and suggests people you should connect with based on whom your contacts know. Also, allow LinkedIn to search your e-mail for contacts. It will ask you which ones to send invitations to, so that you do not have to worry about automatic e-mails being sent to people you'd rather not ask. LinkedIn is like your party host taking you over to meet others who have similar interests.

- *Be a miner.* Mine information that you can take action on. For example, you can receive network updates to get information about what's going on in your network. Recently, an advisor learned about a client who was a corner office executive for Life Science Company in the Northeast, which had been sold. This information prompted a conversation between the advisor and the client. The advisor was able to help the client with his concentrated stock position, which in turn created additional opportunities with the client's colleagues at work. This kind of thing can happen for you if you stay on top of things.

- *Be a giver.* Even though you can't directly solicit through social media, you can share information you think is relevant or meaningful. If you see an interesting article or other relevant information that you want to share with your network, post it on LinkedIn (if it's okay with compliance at your company and with the article's owner). Pushing this kind of thing on people by sending out an e-mail can be annoying, but pulling it by posting it on LinkedIn isn't. Posting it allows the people in your network to discover it on their own and decide for themselves if it's worth reading. Theoretically, the same is true of e-mail, but most people's in-boxes are already so unmanageably large that receiving this kind of unsolicited material is irritating.

Facebook

Facebook is constantly changing. This is the place where your old schoolmates, your new friends, and your family all come together to catch up on what is happening in their lives, show pictures, and post brief status updates to keep you in the loop 24/7. It really feels like your life reunion party. Facebook is not the professional social media medium that LinkedIn is, but if you are going to go on the site, you should know how the best advisors take advantage of their presence here.

Even though your compliance department will not allow you to create a fan page or solicit through social media, Facebook is still a great way to rekindle friendships and get connected to people through people you know. Having a presence on Facebook shows friends, prospects, and clients that you are up with the times and allows you to keep track of what's going on in their lives. Posting on Facebook and responding to posts are acceptable as long as you are giving an opinion and not soliciting. Again, I suggest that you check in with your compliance department for the guidelines it wants you to follow.

Proper Protocol on Facebook

Whether or not you have already put your profile together, here are things you should know and do if you are on Facebook.

- *Be brief.* Subscribe to the KISS (keep it simple, stupid) method. This truism applies here more than you could ever imagine. Tell people about your personal life and a bit about your professional life. The social setting is going to set the tone for this introduction.
- *Be recognizable.* Your profile is representing you. Even though you can't solicit, it is useful as a way for people to learn about you. Because its focus is on the personal and social, and not the professional, it is best used by advisors as a source of insight for potential clients about the kind of person they are.
- *Be consistent.* This helps establish your "brand." Get connected to people, join groups if it is appropriate and acceptable to compliance, and communicate regularly. Communicating regularly could be responding to a post or providing an opinion on topical issues. The key here is that you're entitled to share your perspective as long as you are not soliciting.
- *Be authentic.* Be truthful and kind—never, ever lie, gossip about others (whether what you say is true or not), or exaggerate. What you post can have a huge impact on your personal and professional reputation, so be careful. Before you hit the "Send" button, take another look at what you've written, give it a few minutes, reread it, and if you still like it, send it. Remember, the people you are communicating with are connected to you either directly or through a network of people you know, so think twice before you post.
- *Be cool.* Do not try to force the action. Make sure your profile is not all business and self-promotion. Let your

personality come out, and share things that perhaps even your professional colleagues may not know. Jed, an advisor who is also a musician, is in a band that plays at clubs around the country. He uses Facebook to let people know when and where his group is playing, and countless friends and business associates have attended the shows. Now more people know this about Jed, and it has become a quite a conversation piece.

Twitter

Twitter is like speed dating—you have 140 characters or less to make an impression, drop a comment, or ask a question. It is an excellent tool for gathering and receiving up-to-the-minute intelligence that may come from an industry expert that you hold in high regard, an article from the *Wall Street Journal*, and so on. It is a place where advisors can receive up-to-the-minute information from news and industry sources they choose to follow. It is not a tool that you can use to send information, because compliance departments usually prohibit a professional presence on Twitter.

ORGANIZE YOUR LISTS

When you begin creating and working your lists, you are going to find yourself extremely busy calling people, scheduling meetings, going on more prospective client calls, and constantly adding to your network of contacts. You need to keep everything well organized so that you use your time efficiently and effectively. You have the pertinent information in one place (your contact list)—keep that organized and up-to-date. Otherwise, things will start to slip through the cracks, and you will cease to be effective.

You need to treat every piece of information with equal care, because each piece is equally important. You never know who or what will point you to your next big success (your next big client), so you can't afford to lose track of even one piece of information. Every lead, whether it's small, is from an unpromising source, or seems to be a long shot, must be treated with extreme care. You simply never know where an opportunity is lurking. The lead you lose could be the one!

Defining the Fields

- *Client.* Your active clients.
- *Contact.* Make sure the person's name is spelled correctly. When you can, check this—even if you know the person fairly well. Names are easy to misspell.
- *A, B, C, or D.* Some advisors create separate sheets for As, Bs, Cs, and Ds. Some color-code them. One I know classified all contacts as gold, silver, platinum, or copper. It does not matter how you mark the categories; the important thing is to categorize each contact.
- *Phone number.* Make sure it is correct. Attention to this kind of detail is crucial.
- *E-mail address.* There are many ways an e-mail can go astray. Be especially careful here, and make sure you have the proper spelling and address. Too many times people assume that they have the correct information, but the

e-mail never reaches the recipient and they may never find out. Take the time to ask and get it right.

- *Referral(s).* Keeping track of these referrals is critical. If a referral gives you additional names, put the person's name in the contact field and put the names she gives you to contact in the referral field. As an example, Holly Stone, a referral, gives you the name of Jeffrey Jones to call. Holly now gets placed in the contact field, and Jeffrey is ... that's right, placed in the referral field.
- *Company.* Where your contact, client, or referral works.
- *Title, if known.* You must have this before you contact the individual.
- *Comments.* This is a very important field. As soon as you hang up the phone, write down the essence of your conversation—as you get busy, it will be almost impossible to remember what was said. So don't neglect to do this. Having the information handy, right in your contact list, makes it easy for you to refresh your memory and knowledge of the referral. You can also look at the chronology of all the conversations you've had with an individual, which shows you how well you're doing. So, get in the habit of making careful notes as soon as you hang up!

  Remember, it is *very* easy to lose track of things. Do not rely on your memory. A conversation is never as fresh in your mind 10 days later as it is just after it ended. If you are working your network of contacts correctly, every phone call or visit will trigger a future activity. The bigger your network is, the more important this field becomes.
- *Action to be taken.* If you record this information accurately, you will always know the status of each relationship on your list.

- *Date of initial contact.* It is important that you enter the date for every communication you have. You cannot possibly keep track of the status of all your activities in your head. Timing is crucial when you're making repeat calls or sending out e-mails. If you haven't recorded the dates of your calls, meetings, and e-mails, you will lose track of when you did what. You may call people too soon or too late, and that can throw the whole process off. So always record the dates!

Contact Form Example

Now that you know the kind of information you need, take your list of contacts and enter their essential information in the contact form. I've done one as an example so that you can see what it looks like. The sample format in Table 2-1 is a guideline for storing, organizing, and increasing your network of contacts.

I recommend the use of contact management software because the technology will remind you to do things such as call people. However, if you do not have access to or can't afford to invest in a software package, you can use an Excel spreadsheet and put in these fields.

WHERE YOU ARE NOW

If you've been following the suggestions in each chapter as you read, you now have a clear objective, a supportive strategy, and accountability incorporated into your plan. You have made your contact list, categorized everyone you know, entered the essential information for each person, and think you know whom you want to call.

However, you will make a better impression and get better results if you prepare for the call first. You still have a little more front-end work to do. The next chapter walks you through everything you need to do before you make that important first call.

Table 2-1 Sample Contact Form

Name	Phone Number	E-mail	Referral(s)	Company	Title, If Known	Phone Number	Comments	Action to Be Taken	Date
Michael Saltz	508-555-0000	Msaltz@ msn.com	Lou Lazar	Eleco	President	781-555-0000	Michael gave me three names. He's calling all three for me to set it up	One, call Michael next week to see if he got through to everyone. Two, call his contacts the 2nd	July 12
			Carl Berklund	Myte Security	VP of Finance	508-555-0000			
			Karen Carlson	System Works	VP of marketing	978-555-0000			

3

Asking for Introductions and Getting What You Want

SALMON SAYS
"What you say and, more important, how and when you say it will make all the difference in the world."

Al wanted help getting five of his biggest clients to give him warm introductions. He wanted to ask for these introductions during his quarterly reviews with them. In the past, he hadn't been able to get what he wanted at meetings like this—the problem was in the way he'd been asking.

We agreed on a new strategy and script, and we decided that he'd try it out first on Richard, an A client and a real estate developer. First, when Al called Richard to set up their lunch review, he ended with,

"I'm working on some things here, and I'd like to get your opinion over lunch—would that be okay?"

As expected, Richard said yes. Then, at the beginning of lunch—within five minutes of sitting down, but after the pleasantries—Al reviewed the agenda, ending with,

"As I mentioned on the call to set up our lunch, after we complete the review today, I want to take 5 to 10 minutes to brainstorm with you on something I am working on. Is that still okay?"

Again, Richard said yes, and at the end of the meal, Al said,

"Richard, as I mentioned, I'd like to bounce an idea off of you. Can we still do that?"

Richard agreed, and Al responded with,

"Great. I want to talk with you now, businessperson to businessperson. I know you have a recipe for success, and like you, I run my practice with a clear business model. It includes developing more relationships with other successful real estate people. I'd like to meet these people through people I know. You've mentioned people like this before, so I know you run in those circles. If you were me, how would you suggest I go about meeting them?"

Richard nodded and immediately offered to introduce Al to two successful real estate developers.

At this point, most advisors think, "Whew! I asked; he offered to make an introduction; I am done." Wrong. You have done most of the heavy lifting, but you still need to get your contact or client to commit to when and how he is going to do what he promised. If you don't get that commitment when you ask, you will be waiting a long time for an introduction.

Al did not miss a beat. Right after Richard offered to make those two introductions, Al said,

"How do you want to do this? Should the four of us play golf or have lunch, or do you want to give me their contact information and I will call them? Tell me what you are comfortable doing and what's best for you as to when it happens."

Al was successful for four reasons. He knew:

- *Whom to ask.* Richard was a good choice because he was an A client who had already offered to make an introduction on Al's behalf.
- *When to ask.* Al's timing was perfect: he staged, framed, and asked sequentially, so that the request flowed naturally from the conversation and didn't seem to come out of left field.
- *How to ask.* Al's execution—the way he asked—was courteous and kept everything relaxed. Al asked Richard if he was okay with the request, which made it easy for Richard to say no if he wanted to. Al was specific about what he wanted, which made it easy for Richard to think of people to whom he could introduce Al.
- *What to ask for.* Lastly, Al did not let Richard off the hook. By asking Richard how he wanted to proceed, Al ensured that what they'd agreed to would really happen and virtually guaranteed the outcome that he wanted. Throughout the conversation, Al made Richard comfortable, earned the opportunity to ask, and sounded logical and practical. I doubt that Richard ever felt that Al was pressing him—the conversation went through a natural progression of best next steps. In this chapter, you will learn how to set things up so that your requests go through these steps, too.

Another advisor, Leah, told me that she always felt uncomfortable asking clients for referrals and knew that she sounded as awkward as she felt. She knew she needed to ask, but she sensed that her requests were coming out of nowhere and left everyone feeling uneasy. This was typical. At the end of a phone conversation with an A client, Fred, an executive at a publicly traded company, Leah nervously said,

"Fred, we have been working together for many years now, and I know you are happy with the service I have provided you and your family, and I really enjoy working with you. I am looking to expand my practice and wanted to ask if you can think of anyone you know who could benefit from my services."

Fred said, "No one comes to mind."

Leah gracefully thanked him for the thought and dropped the subject. Of course, she felt terrible for having asked. As she said to me:

"This is why I don't ask for referrals. I hate the anxiety I have when I ask, and I never get the response I want."

I told her that she was not alone; many advisors feel uncomfortable asking clients for referrals. I shared Al's story to show her that he changed this dynamic and she could, too. So can you, if you follow the who, when, how, and what sequence.

WHEN TO ASK

Once you know whom you're going to ask, you need to make sure you set up your request sequentially to get the outcome you want. Follow the stage, frame, deliver formula in chronological order, as Al did, and your chances of success will vastly improve.

Staging and Framing—Setting an Expectation

If you are planning to ask in person, set up and prepare for your request over the phone by letting people know that something in addition to their business will be discussed at the meeting. I suggest phone and not e-mail because people can't hear your inflections in an e-mail, and when you say something like, "I want to take 5 or 10 minutes to bounce an idea off of you," or "I'd like to brainstorm with you about something I'm working on; is that okay?" you need people to hear those inflections.

Nine out of 10 times, people say will yes to this kind of question if you ask over the phone. Of course, if a client has told you that he prefers e-mail, you have to ask that way— but I have found that the phone works better.

Just setting things up this way goes a long way toward allaying anxiety. Letting people know that something is coming at the end of a client review meeting means that both parties are prepared for it. The preparation may also pique your client's interest: many people like to be asked for favors.

When you begin the meeting, go over the agenda and remind your client that at the end you want to cover some things, as discussed on the phone, and ask if that's still okay. When Al did this, he said it made him feel even more relaxed—a huge weight was lifted off his shoulders because he had the client's permission to ask.

Framing the meeting up front and confirming with the client not only allays anxiety, it allows you to stay focused on the task at hand and not get distracted or worried by thinking about the "ask" portion of your meeting when you should be listening to your client and addressing his concerns. If you set things up properly, your request will come as a natural part of the conversation.

If your ask is going to take place over the phone, you set it up and frame it differently. Start the conversation with an exchange of pleasantries before you ask if it is a good time to speak, and make sure you ask about the other person. The last thing you want to do is come across as desperate or interested only in what your client or contact can do for you. Begin with something simple, such as:

- "How are you doing?"
- "What's happening?"
- "How is everyone at home?"
- "How have you been?"

These pleasantries should last no more than five minutes. You do not want to get so involved in another conversation that asking for a referral sounds like an afterthought.

Next, check to make sure it's a good time. Say something along the lines of:

- Do you have a few more minutes (if this comes after the pleasantries)?

- Am I getting you at a good time?
- I was thinking about you the other day, as I am working on some things here. Do you have five minutes to talk?
- I am working on some things here, and they made me think of you. I want to bounce an idea off of you. Can we do that now?

You may also want to ask for a specific amount of time. Leah admitted that this was something she had never asked clients or contacts prior to our work together. Once she started doing this, she told me that the tone of her clients and contacts changed and they were more receptive when she just asked that simple question.

Most advisors fail to ask this question and simply leap ahead into their "pitch," only to find out that the person is busy or is rushing out to a meeting. You will have lost all momentum, and if you get a chance to repeat your spiel later on, your chances of success will have greatly diminished. Don't let that happen. Make sure you have the person's undivided attention before you actually ask for the referral—if you sense that she's distracted in any way, ask another time.

Delivery

The timing of your ask is just as important as what you say. If you're going to ask during a review at a meal, as Al did, the best time for you to broach the subject is either right before or right after dessert.

Begin your meeting or meal with pleasantries, such as what's going on in the client's life personally, current events, sports, and the like. This humanizes things and reinforces the fact that your relationship is personal as well as professional.

Next, go through the review. It is important that you cover this first because it's why your client is meeting you. Your ask is secondary, and covering the client's needs first shows respect and proves that you are someone who can and does put other people first. After you have covered all the things that both of you planned to discuss, and the client is comfortable with what was discussed and agreed upon, you are ready for the ask.

If you are going to ask over the phone, as Leah did, the best time to ask is right after the client agrees to speak to you at that time. Be focused, succinct, and specific. Many advisors feel they need to remind their clients of all the great work they have done for them as a windup to the actual ask. That is not necessary.

The person is your client because you do a great job for him and have a strong relationship with him. You do not need to remind him of that in this conversation. What you do need to do is help him visualize exactly what your target account profile is. If you create a clear image of the kind of people you want to meet, your client can start thinking of people he knows who fit the description. The clearer you are, the easier that will be.

HOW TO ASK

People can sense when you are reading a canned speech or saying something that isn't genuine. This is true whether you are on the phone or talking in person. Have you ever been on the receiving end of one of those canned pitches? If you have, you know how people react to them: we all want to end the conversation as quickly as possible.

The Cheese Factor—Phrases to Avoid

There are several phrases that create anxiety, or even angst, in a conversation. Don't use them, ever! Eliminate these lines from your ask:

- "Do you know any people who may have a need for my services?"
- "Can you think of people you know who could benefit from my services?"
- "Can you think of anyone who could benefit from my services?"
- "Do you have any friends or family members that you can introduce me to?"
- "Who do you know that you think would want to know about me?"
- "Do you know anyone who is looking for a financial advisor?"
- "I want to work with people who have substantial wealth. Can you think of someone you know who's like that whom you can introduce me to?"
- "I want to work with more high-net-worth clients. Can you think of someone you know who's like that whom you can introduce me to?"

Leah once used all of these phrases. Have you ever used any of them? What kind of reaction did you get? If such a request didn't work out for you, I am not surprised. The other person was probably thinking something like, "Wow, you are making me go through a mental hoop. I'm really uncomfortable. I feel I am being put on the spot, but he's asking, so who do I know that has a lot of money? Wait, how much is a lot of money? Hm . . . yeah, I can give Jack . . . ooh, I better not; he wouldn't want to be put on the spot like this either, and he'll get mad at me for giving his name out."

Naturally, when people react this way to your request, you don't get referrals. The other person feels uncomfortable and doesn't want his friends to feel uncomfortable, too.

Be Specific and Make Them Feel Comfortable

Most advisors think that if they're too specific about the people they want to meet, they'll be limiting their opportunities. In reality, the more vague you are, the harder it is for people to think of referrals. Vague requests are rarely honored. The more focused and specific you are, the more likely you are to succeed. Here are examples of the new, more specific asks that Leah used that produced tremendous results for her:

- "I want to develop more relationships with doctors, and I want to meet those doctors through a warm introduction. That being said, would you be comfortable either introducing me to or giving me the contact information for two or three doctors you know just so that they are aware of me as a resource?"

- "I want to meet Joe Russo, and I want to meet him through people I know. Would you be comfortable setting something up for the three of us to get together so that I can get to know him?"
- "I know you know Joe Russo. Would you be comfortable making an introduction on my behalf just so that he is aware of me as a resource?"
- "I want to meet more business owners through a warm introduction, and I thought of you because I know you run in those circles. Are there two or three business owners you know that you'd feel comfortable introducing me to just so that they are aware of me as a resource?"

Those descriptions made the kind of person Leah wanted to meet crystal clear. There was no mystery as to what she wanted. In addition, using the phrase "you'd feel comfortable introducing me to" makes the client or contact feel that the choice of whom she introduces you to is now hers, on her terms. This is very different from the way people feel when they are asked one of the "cheese factor" questions!

Lastly, the phrase "just so that they are aware of me as a resource" gives your client or contact the feeling that it will be okay to make introductions on your behalf. You will not be aggressive, let alone give their friends a shakedown.

Asking this way was a game changer for Leah. As I told her, "If you ask with sincerity and confidence, you're probably going to get what you want." But before you can do this, you may need to work on your mindset, as Leah did. She felt that asking for a referral was a sign of weakness and that she would be viewed as desperate and needy if she did it.

Does that thought run across your mind? If it does, you're looking at it backward. Ask yourself the questions I asked Leah.

"Do you think you are good at what you do?"

Leah hesitated and then said, "Yes."

"Is there anybody else you would want managing your clients' money?"

This is where Leah got animated. With conviction, she emphatically said, "No." I asked her if she really believed this, and again, in a louder voice, she said, "Yes."

Do you feel the same way? If you do, remember that successful people understand that success comes as much from whom they know as from what they know. Successful people did not get where they are without having introductions made on their behalf and doors opened for them. They're constantly expanding their own networks, and they know you need to expand yours. An important part of their power base is their own network, which they rely on for things like tickets to a ball game, good tables at restaurants, and introductions.

As we talked, Leah got it, too. She started to see the value in asking and changed her approach to the whole topic. Changing yours—really believing in the value of your work, your value to your clients, and that they will be happy to honor that value by making introductions for you—is the only way you will be able to make things work for you. So get that mindset, approach these opportunities with confidence and conviction, and ask the way Leah did.

If all else fails, ask yourself: what is the worst that can happen? Someone says no. That may happen, but if you have this mindset and use the scripts in this chapter, the odds are in your favor that it won't.

WHAT TO DO AFTER YOU'VE ASKED

So let's say you've asked, and the person has given you a name—then what? Do you breathe a sigh of relief, say thank you, and end the conversation? Absolutely not: remember Al.

Get a Commitment for When and How

All your previous efforts will be wasted if you skip this last step: getting a commitment for when and how the introduction will take place. Getting people to do what they say they will do *without feeling pressured* requires tact, skill, and the right attitude.

As soon as someone agrees to make an introduction on your behalf, a bell should go off in your head telling you that it's time to push a little further. When you hear it, obey it, knowing that you not only have earned the right to ask for more, but have been given permission to do so. Say something like:

- "How do you want to do this?"
- "What do you suggest as next steps?"
- "When do you want me to get back to you on this?"
- "Thanks very much. I really appreciate that. How do you want to proceed?"
- "When do you want to do that?"

- "What works best with your schedule?"
- "When should I get back to you on this?"
- "When will you get back to me on setting that up?"
- "What do you think is the best way to make this happen, and when do you want to do this?"
- "How do you suggest we do this, and what did you have in mind for a day and time?"
- "How do you want to do this? Do you want to set up golf or a meal, do you want to call, or do you want to give me his contact information and I will call?"
- "You tell me what's best for you and when you can make it happen."

Al started being more assertive using these phrases, and he told me, "This nonthreatening way you taught me to get commitments from contacts and clients made a difference in moving the process along. I have so many more opportunities now, just from this one tip."

Al's clients and contacts became more responsive to him because of the way he asked. The questions just given ensure that clients and contacts will both do what they say they'll do *and* tell you how and when they're comfortable doing it. In fact, the whole process becomes even more acceptable to them because you've put them in control of the introduction. This ensures their support and increases the likelihood that things will happen as planned.

When contacts and clients give their advisor a verbal contract, most of them keep it. Human nature is such that people generally do not renege on those types of contract commitments. Once a client has given you one, wrap things up. You want what was mutually agreed upon to be the last thing she remembers about the conversation. If you keep talking, you run the risk of talking your client or contact out of doing what she said she would do for you, or making it easy for her to forget what she promised.

BEING PREPARED FOR THE WHAT-IFS
OF A CONTACT OR CLIENT CONVERSATION

This section will show you what to do in various situations you may encounter when asking for introductions.

What If Someone Offers to Make the Call for You?

What you should do in this case depends upon who the person is. When my father, for example, offered to tell his advisor about me, I knew that wasn't a good idea. My father doesn't know what I do—he thinks I'm a career counselor.

People who know you but don't know what you do may have good intentions, but it's usually not a good idea to let them represent you in the marketplace. Have them give you the referral's contact information and call the person yourself.

If you can't do that without hurting their feelings, do what I did with my father: thank them, let them know how much you appreciate their kind offer, and then ask if you can forward them a few bullet-point pieces of information. Say something like, "Before I meet people through a mutual friend, I find it usually works best if they know something about me and heard it from you. Would you mind if I sent you just a little information that you can use when you speak to . . . ?"

Then, ask if you can call back once they've received the information to see if they're comfortable communicating it to the referral. This is a great way to ensure that you get the outcome you want. I sent my father an e-mail with three simple bullet points about my work and asked him to refer to it the next time he wants to let people know about me. It has helped.

However, if you are confident that the person making the offer can articulate what you do and how you do it (perhaps better than you can yourself!), by all means, let her make that initial call on your behalf. You can even ask her to! What's the worst that can happen? She can decline, and you are no worse off than you were before.

People will respect you for having the temerity to ask. Asking is perfectly acceptable, as long as you maintain a polite, professional, confident manner. Successful people know that networking is a two-way street and that some day you may well be in a position to return the favor.

What If You Are Not Sure Where You Stand at Any Point During the Conversation?

If at any time during the conversation you are not sure where you stand, stop and say something like,

- "What are you thinking?"
- "What do you think?"
- "How does that sound to you?"
- "Are we okay here?"
- "Would you be comfortable . . . ?"

This way you'll know where you stand, eliminate any doubt, and be able to continue with a clear mind and focus.

What If Things Do Not Go as Planned?

Sometimes you ask and get a no. Sometimes you're talking and you sense that things are not going well. When these things happen, it could be because the person is just not open to the idea of making introductions on your behalf. It could be that he's just not comfortable with the concept, period. It could also be because of the way you asked. Whatever the reason, you have only two options: drop it or pursue it further. To drop it, say something along the lines of:

- "I appreciate the time and your candor. No problem."

If you want to probe a little further because of the strength of the relationship and/or you want to know why your client or contact's is hesitating, ask:

- "What more would I need to do to get you comfortable with making a warm introduction on my behalf?"

What If You Get an Objection?

Even time-tested scripts aren't bulletproof. No matter where the scripts come from, none of them will ever guarantee that you will get an introduction every time you ask for one. That being said, when the receiver of your message raises objections, you must respond with confidence in order to have a chance of turning him around.

There are two types of objections, implicit and explicit. When your contact, client, or referral looks uncomfortable, avoids your eyes, or tries to change the subject, you're probably getting an implicit objection. When this happens, look him in the eye and say something along the lines of, "I sense that there is some hesitation on your part here or that you are not comfortable having this conversation. Am I reading the situation right?" This will allow you to get a reaction one way or the other so that you know exactly where you stand and find out what your client or contact is actually thinking.

When your client or referral just comes out and says that she's not interested, not comfortable making the introduction, or whatever, you're getting an explicit objection.

Here are the most common explicit objections advisors hear and ways to respond to them:

"I want to preserve the confidentiality we have."

"I want you to know that I respect and value the confidentiality of our association, and you should know that I truly take it to heart. Let me ask a question if I may. Do you feel I have done anything in our time together that would give you cause for concern? Please know that I would treat any referral you give me with the same care and trust we have established, and I would never breach that trust and the friendship we have. Just think for a minute how we were introduced. Without _____ calling you on my behalf, we would never have had the opportunity to work together, and I wouldn't have been able to build the kind of practice I have with people like yourself, who make what I do so meaningful. I would take the same low-key advice-driven approach with anyone you introduce me to."

"Giving a referral makes me uncomfortable."

"Please know that I am not asking you to give me a list of your friends to call. I would never do that. I want to meet people who are more [fill in the blank with your profile of the person] through a warm introduction just so that they are aware of me as a resource, and if you know someone like that and you would be comfortable introducing me to her, I would love to meet her. I realize it is up to her whether she decides to meet with me or not."

"I don't know anyone's situation, and I'm unsure if my friends are looking for someone to work with."

"I am not asking you to introduce me to your friends or share intimate information about anyone you would suggest I contact. Here is my profile of the type of people I like to work with. [Give your profile of your ideal client.] Now that you know the type of people I want to meet through a warm introduction, if you feel comfortable making that connection for me, I would really appreciate it. If there is a connection and it turns out that we end up working together, please know that I will handle things with the sensitivity, empathy, grace, and care I have given our relationship."

"I will have to give this more thought."

"I understand. I treat referrals like they are gold, and I am very selective as to whom I would refer someone to, so I can relate to what you are saying. What would be a good day and time for us to circle back and revisit this?"

Every request, and the stages leading up to it, must be managed in a certain way if you are to extract promises and get your clients, contacts, and referrals to do what you want them to do for you.

TIME-TESTED SCRIPTS TO GET THE JOB DONE

You now understand the process; here are actual scripts, containing the crucial words and phrases that will enable you to get the outcomes you want.

Example 1: Asking a Client for a Warm Introduction over the Telephone

"John, it is Mitchell. How are you doing? How are Nancy and the kids doing?"

Continue with:

"I was thinking about you the other day as I was working on some things here. Do you have a few minutes?"

Or,

"Am I getting you at a good time?"

If the client says no, continue with:

"Is there a better day and time for us to speak? Please let me know what's best for you."

If the client says yes, to meet more people that meet your profile, continue with:

"I want to meet more _____ [fill in the blank with information from your profile: business owners, corner office executives, retirees, or some other group, and/or mirror the person you are speaking with: attorney, doctor, widow, or whatever] through people I know."

Or,

"I want to develop relationships with more _____ [fill in the blank with information from your profile: business owners, corner office executives, retirees, or some other group, and/or mirror the person you are speaking with: attorney, doctor, widow, or whatever].

"And I want to meet them through warm introductions made on my behalf."

Or,

"And I want to meet them through people I know."

Continue with:

"That being said, would you be comfortable either introducing me to or giving me the contact information for two or three people you know that fit my profile just so that they are aware of me as a resource?"

For an introduction to someone specific, continue with:

"I want to meet Rachel Strong, and I want to meet her through people I know. Would you be comfortable setting something up for the three of us to get together so that I can get to know her?"

Or you can say:

"I know you know Rachel Strong. Would you be comfortable making an introduction on my behalf, just so that she is aware of me as a resource?"

Whether you ask by profile or by name, continue with either:

"Do you want to set it up for a meal or golf, do you want to call, or you do you just want to give me her contact information and I will call?"

Or:

"You tell me what's best for you and when you can make it happen."

If your client says yes, you may ask either of these questions:

"How well do you know Rachel?"

"If you were me, how would you approach Rachel?"

Example 2: Asking a Contact for a Warm Introduction over the Telephone.

This kind of conversation requires more explanation and more details about what you want the other person to do. It also gives the other person an easy way to say either yes or no without feeling pressured or uncomfortable.

After you get through the pleasantries (the small talk about personal things like family, friends, what the person did socially recently, and so on), begin with:

> "John, I was thinking about you the other day as I was working on some things here. I want to talk about business and could use your help, okay?"

Or:

> "John, I am working on some things here, and it made me think of you. I want to bounce an idea off of you. Can we do that?"

Continue with:

> "Is this a good time for you?" (If he says no, follow the directions from Exercise 1.)

"As I looked at where I've had the greatest success with new clients over the past few years, it has been through warm introductions. And, I want to develop more relationships with people who have sold their business a few times, corporate executives, and retired corporate executives through warm introductions made on my behalf.

"As I reflected on my strategy, it made me think of you because I know you run in these circles. I also truly value our friendship, and I don't want to overstep my boundaries because our friendship means everything to me.

"With that being said, my question to you is this: would you be comfortable introducing me to people you know who fit my profile just so that they are aware of me as a resource?"

Or:

"If you were me, how would you go about it?"

If the contact says yes, *do not forget to ask questions such as*:

"How do you suggest we do this? Do you want to set up a meal or golf, do you want to call, or do you just want to give me his contact information and I will call?"

"What do you think is the best way to make this happen?"

"When should I get back to you on this?"

Example 3: Asking a Client for a Warm Introduction in Person, After Either a Review or a Meal

After the pleasantries, begin by saying:

> "When we scheduled our meeting, I mentioned that we would cover a review of your statements, some ideas on rebalancing, and the other things you wanted to discuss today. In addition, I said that at the end, I wanted to bounce a business idea off of you. Is that still okay with you?"

Then have your review and/or meal—don't say anything else about your request until you have finished. Then, when you have finished the review or, if the conversation is taking place over a meal, when you have ordered dessert or are having coffee, say:

> "As I mentioned earlier, I am working on some things, and I wanted to bounce a business idea off of you. Can we do that now?"

Depending on the relationship you have with your client and what feels comfortable, you can say:

> "I want to meet more real estate developers through people I know."

Or:

"I want to meet more real estate developers through a warm introduction."

Or:

"I want to develop more relationships with real estate developers, and I want to do it through a warm introduction."

Or:

"I want to develop more relationships with real estate developers, and I want to meet them through people I know."

Or:

"I want to develop more relationships with real estate developers, and I want to meet them through people I know who would be comfortable making a warm introduction on my behalf."

Regardless of which option you choose, continue with:

"If you were me, how would you suggest I go about that?"

Or:

"My question is this: would you be comfortable making an introduction to one or two real estate developers on my behalf just so that they are aware of me as a resource?"

If the client says yes, *do not forget to ask questions such as*:

"How do you suggest we do this? Do you want to set up a meal or golf, do you want to call, or do you just want to give me the contact information and I will call?"

"What do you think is the best way to make this happen?"

"When should I get back to you on this?"

"How well do you know _____?"

"If you were me, how would you approach _____?"

If you do not receive the answer you were looking for, then say something like:

"That's a good thought. I was thinking about doing it this way: _____. How does that sound?"

POST-CONVERSATION ADVICE:
GIVE YOURSELF SOME FEEDBACK

After the conversation, spend some time assessing how it went. Whether it went well or not so well, doing this will help you grow more comfortable with and better at making requests. Go through the following checklist, answering all the questions in as much detail as you can, to see how well you did.

- Did you personalize and customize the conversation?
- Did you have a call objective? In other words, did you have a distinct purpose for the call or conversation?

- Did you make it easy for this person to do what you wanted her to do?
- Did you remember not to "let him off the hook"?
- Did she commit to doing something for you?
- Was your objective for the conversation satisfied?

If you can answer yes to all of these questions, you are well on your way to stuffing your pipeline with countless warm referral introductions, as Al and Leah did.

Al and Leah's use of this process has made a huge difference to the quality and velocity of their business development. By using the stage, frame, deliver method, they have exceeded their net new asset goals year after year. It all came down to having a better way of approaching people, a way that gave both of them more confidence. The positive reactions and feedback they received led to a little more success, which gave them still more confidence.

They took what we'd worked on, incorporated it into their own personalities, and made it their own. Finding their own voices made the process feel even more right and natural. My parting piece of advice to them both was, "Do more of it."

As you look at the time-tested scripts of successful advisors in this chapter, adapt them to your own personality and style. Once they feel right to you, you too will have the kind of success at getting referrals that Al and Leah are now enjoying. The next chapter shows you how to prepare for talking to those referrals.

4

Prepping to Make
a Great Impression

SALMON SAYS

"Treat each new introduction like pure gold. You can't just wing it."

When Kristen, a seasoned advisor at a New Jersey wire house, had lunch with a prospective client, she didn't even mention business. Instead, she concentrated on getting to know Stephanie on a personal level, as instructed by the friend who had introduced them. Stephanie was a female executive in the cosmetics industry, and the two women found a great deal to discuss.

Later, the mutual friend called Kristin.

"Stephanie really liked you—and now she wants to talk to you about her portfolio."

Thrilled, Kristin was about to call Stephanie, but, luckily, she called me instead.

"Hold on," I said. "Is anything happening in Stephanie's world that's driving this interest?"

73

*Kristin didn't know, but after our talk, she found out. Steph-
anie had just experienced a liquidity event and had $6 million
to invest. Kristin had worked with two other female executives
in the cosmetics industry who had experienced liquidity events.
She also learned that Stephanie was interviewing two other
brokerage firms.*

*"Make sure you communicate your experience with women in
the cosmetics industry early in the conversation," I said.*

*So when Kristin called Stephanie, she concisely explained her
experience with other female executives in the cosmetics industry
who had experienced liquidity events, using substantive real-life
examples.*

*Not surprisingly, Stephanie chose Kristin as her advisor—
to the tune of $18 million (the other $12 million came from
Stephanie's husband). When Kristin later asked why she had
been chosen, Stephanie said, "The other advisors took me to their
offices, introduced me to everyone, and in general rolled out the
red carpet. You demonstrated that you knew my world."*

Be like Kristin: prepare properly before you have that
first conversation with a contact or referral. Only by doing
your research can you sound credible and create the best possible impression of yourself and your work. As they say in the
military, "You need the G-2 intelligence" to put yourself in
the best position to win.

Getting that intelligence—doing your homework—puts
you one step ahead of most advisors, who wing it. Don't be
one of them! You get only one chance to make a good first
impression—don't squander it the way Sam did.

Sam was well known in parts of Alabama and wanted to
expand his business in Birmingham—especially his business

with partners at law firms. He knew that he and Lori, the managing partner of a law firm with more than 100 employees, had a mutual friend. So Sam called this friend, who gave him permission to call Lori and use his name.

As soon as they'd hung up, Sam called Lori and said,

"Arnold suggested I contact you. I'd like to come and see you and tell you all about our organization and how we do things, and what we can do for you and your firm. In advance, I'd like to send you some information about us [aka a pitch book] that goes into detail about many things you may want to know about us. Would that be okay?"

That was all he said! Lori liked and respected Arnold, so she agreed, but Sam had not made a good impression. He called her several times to get on her calendar, but it never happened. They never even met.

Sam blew it with Lori in two ways. First, he gave her no compelling reasons for possibly working with him. Worse, he made the conversation all about him, without demonstrating that he understood her world, her firm, or anything about her personally. He didn't even show any interest in her.

Sam squandered this introduction. A personal introduction is simply that—an introduction. That is all: it opens the door, but whether or not you get in the door is up to you. How you prepare for that initial conversation and how you conduct yourself during the actual conversation determine whether the Arnolds in your network will make more introductions for you and whether referrals like Lori will meet with you.

Kristin's success was not an accident. She followed a strategy. First, she figured out what information was critical and found it. Then she matched her own and her organization's strengths with her new knowledge of the referral's hot buttons, the things that were truly important to Stephanie. Kristin used that calibration in her conversation with Stephanie.

This chapter shows you how to do what Kristin did, step by step. If you follow the steps, your contacts will open more doors for you than you ever imagined they could, and the odds of success will be in your favor.

BEGIN WITH YOUR ATTITUDE

Overall, 90 percent of advisors admit that they do little, if any, prep work before calling a referral. Thus, doing the prep work will put you in the top 10 percent of advisors, the ones who make favorable impressions. The up-front work you do will go a long way toward getting you where you ultimately want to be with these prospective clients. How you conduct yourself in that first interaction will set the tone for future conversations—in fact, it will even determine whether there are future conversations. That's why it's so important that you invest the time on the front end doing your homework. When you know as much as you can, when you've gathered as much information as possible, you're far more likely to make a favorable impression. You need to come across as knowledgeable, empathetic, credible, resourceful, and organized.

That starts with your attitude. First, look at each and every situation as a unique opportunity. Realize that people do business with you for two main reasons: because they like you and because they trust you. Your clients liked and trusted you when they hired you, and over time you have reinforced those feelings through your actions. What you did got results and gave your clients the satisfaction of knowing that their portfolios were where they wanted them to be. Your actions are an integral part of why they continue to work with you, because you have given them peace of mind.

In establishing a new relationship, start by getting enough information to understand something about the referral's personal and professional situation. For example, maybe he is frustrated with his current advisor, or he likes to talk about his family before discussing business—it's your job to find that out before you talk. The more you know about the referral before you have that first contact, the more you'll know about what will work and the more confident you will be.

That confidence will have a direct impact. Basketball great Michael Jordan always had a winning attitude because he was prepared and believed in his abilities. When the ball went up for the game, you expected the Bulls to win every one of them. So did Michael. He brought that attitude to every game. People gravitate to confident, positive people. Your positive attitude is infectious and contagious and helps make a great first impression. Carry yourself with that confidence and attitude, and more referrals will want to be a part of your team.

Besides, the more confident you are, the more relaxed you will be, and the more relaxed you are, the better you will listen and the easier it will be to follow the old adage, "Be yourself." Listening and being yourself will do more than anything else to establish a good relationship early on and enable you to develop the same rapport you have with your current clients.

IDENTIFY WHAT YOU NEED TO KNOW

Before you make the phone call or go to the meeting, answer these three basic questions. If you don't know the answers to these questions, you are not ready to pursue an opportunity with this person professionally during your initial conversation, whether it is by phone or in person. You get only one chance to make a first impression, and first impressions are lasting. The last thing you want to do is go unprepared and set the wrong tone. You are better off taking a pass until you feel comfortable and confident that you are ready.

1. *What does this person do and/or what industry is she in?* The answer to this question may be fairly simple and easy to obtain. Kristin, for example, knew that Stephanie was a senior vice president at Revlon, which is in the cosmetics industry. The answer to this question came from their mutual friend.
2. *Based on what I know about this individual and my area of expertise, what is my value to this person or her organization?* This question will almost certainly take some research. Your contact is usually the first and possibly the best source. Kristin and Stephanie's mutual friend gave Kristin tremendous insight into Stephanie's world. In

Kristin's case, this invaluable information could not have come from any other source, and having it made Kristin more confident and relaxed during the conversation. It also helped her prepare her answers to the third basic question. You should do this, too. When your contact suggests that you call a referral, say thank you and then ask if you can ask a few questions to gain insight into what's going on in the referral's world. Then say something like, "Would that be okay?" or "Can we do that?"

3. *Based on what I know about this person and myself, what do I have to offer that is quantifiable, is measurable, and makes me stand out from the crowd (both personally and professionally)?*

    You can't answer this question until you've researched question 2. In Kristin's case, her value came not only from the rapport she'd established with Stephanie but from her experience with other female executives in the cosmetics industry. She knew enough about them to talk shop and hit their "hot buttons."

    Specifically, Kristin could tell Stephanie that she:

    • Had more than 15 years' experience working with female executives in the cosmetics industry
    • Had handled more than 50 liquidity events for countless clients who were in a situation similar to Stephanie's.

In other words, this was not her first rodeo. As it turned out, the way Kristin was able to articulate these points established the framework for a meaningful relationship and enabled her to separate herself from the other advisors that Stephanie interviewed.

If you do not have the experience to do what Kristin did, look for other common threads from the information you've gathered. It might be your mutual interest in golf, the fact that the referral is a business owner and you work with other business owners, or the fact that you both sit on boards. The point is to identify some connection, as this will distinguish you from the 90 percent of advisors who talk only about themselves and what they can do for the referral.

You may not be ready to answer any of these three questions yet—the rest of the chapter will show you how to get those answers. For now, it's enough to understand the value of knowing as much as you can about an individual or organization with which you want to do business.

GET THE CRITICAL INFORMATION

There are numerous sources for the information you need. Using only one of them may provide you with all of it, or you may need to consult several sources. Start with the person who gave you the referral.

How many times have you been given a referral from someone, said, "Thanks a lot," and, like 90 percent of your colleagues, within minutes (or maybe seconds) called the referral? Continue the conversation with your contact before calling! The person who gave you the referral is typically a great source of information—you will probably learn more about the referral from him than from any other source available to you.

The Person Who Gave You the Referral

I am not suggesting you interrogate this person, or give him the third degree. There are, however, things your contact may know and enjoy sharing with you, such as:

- What the referral is like personally and her interests and hobbies.
- The referral's current situation: is he married, divorced, or widowed, or has anything recently changed for him, either personally or professionally?
- What the referral does professionally.
- Insight into what's going on in the referral's life. Did she recently get a promotion or have a liquidity event like a sale of a business, an inheritance, or a merged practice?
- Insight into what is going on in the referral's company.
- The referral's hot buttons.
- The best way to approach the referral. This is an area that makes some people feel awkward. The best thing to do is just come out and ask: "If you were me, how would you approach Steve?" or "Are there things I should stay away from?"

Having this kind of information gives you an enormous edge in your conversation with the referral, one that capitalizes on the relationship between your contact and your referral. How you sprinkle this information into the conversation will be covered in detail in the next chapter; for now, concentrate on getting the information.

Then capture the information in a place other than your head. Write it down—on a pad, on a profile you create in your database, or in the notes section of your mobile phone. You may think you will remember everything your contact or client told you about the referral, but that's almost impossible, especially if there is a gap of weeks or months before you have that first conversation.

Current or Former Coworkers

People you know who have worked for or with someone, or even people who don't know him but work at the same company, can also give you tremendous insight. Whether they know what the person is like, what the organization is like, or both, they can be enormously helpful. Your ability to ask good questions and gain as much insight as possible will allow you to assess the situation quickly and come up with a game plan to win the business. For example if you are competing for 401(k) business or going after a nonprofit, this will give you a competitive edge and probably improve your chances of having multiple meetings with people at the organization. The more meetings you have, the more you get to develop relationships and increase your chances of winning the business. If you have had one meeting with people in the organization, an individual, or a family before you made a presentation and I have had five, which of us do you think has established a better relationship and is likely get the business?

If you ask good questions, insiders can give you helpful information.

On an Individual or Family

- What is happening at the company and their position
- Changes in the company that may affect things on a personal level

Going After 401(k) and Nonprofit Opportunities

- How the organization is doing
- How it is viewed in its industry
- What makes it so successful
- Its current or future challenges
- Its decision-making process
- Who is involved, what their names are, and their titles or roles
- Timeline for making a decision
- Who else the organization is considering
- What is driving this
- Why the organization wants to make a change

Asking good questions and using the answers will send a strong message that you have done your homework and are different, real, more credible, and more qualified than your competition.

The Internet

Technology has allowed us to gather a tremendous amount of information from the public domain. Once you've gathered information from people, get the big picture from the Internet.

You can sometimes get a full background on the person you're going to be contacting online. In searching for either individuals or companies, these are the search engines and sites that the best advisors use and find especially helpful:

- *LinkedIn.* As mentioned in Chapter 2, this is a great site for getting reconnected with old colleagues professionally, finding people who work in a particular company you are targeting, or looking at your clients' profiles to see if any of them know someone that you want to meet. In addition, you can use this site to identify someone you know by name that you want to meet and see how many degrees of separation it would take through people you know to get a warm introduction to that person.
- *Facebook.* Things change almost on a daily basis, but the few constants are that everyone has a bio and connections. From looking at these two areas, you can pick up some information that you might not get from others, such as interests, hobbies, and family information.
- *Google.* Type in the person's name and see what you come up with. Don't overlook how little most people know—for example, many people don't know that on Google, the order of the words in the search is important. They also don't know that you can use up to 10 words and when to use all of them and when not to.

- *Hoovers.* This site provides great information including a listing of key executives, size, and annual revenues on over 32 million companies all over the world. There is a cost associated with being a member.
- *Bloomberg.* This site is a great source for up-to-the-minute information, "real time" news, and information on companies and industries. This is the best source of information and where the real pros in financial services go for unfiltered and factual reporting without any spin.
- *Search.com.* This site is similar to Google and can be used as an alternative or additional source to search for information on an individual or organization.

The Organization's Website

The information you gain from this source is invaluable. Whether you are targeting companies, nonprofits, or law firms, check their websites. This is a vital part of your due diligence regardless of the amount of other information you have, because it is the medium the organization is using to provide the public with the most updated information it wants you to have about it.

Once you get to the organization's website, be sure to look carefully at:

- *Investor relations.* You can and should look at public companies' financial reports to see how big they are and how well they are doing.
- *Media or press.* This section is key. It will tell you what's happening in terms of new product releases, acquisitions, industry recognition, and changes in senior management.

You will undoubtedly want to be able to acknowledge and discuss this kind of information during both your initial and subsequent discussions.

- *Management team.* This is important because you may find that someone you know is on the team—and if you do, that person could become an important contact. If you don't know anyone, scrutinize the whole team to see if you can find some kind of connection. Then ask your network of contacts what they might know about the team members. More often than you'd think, you will find someone who went to the same college or perhaps worked at a company where you or someone in your network works or worked. If you look hard enough, you can find a connection.

Its Competitors' Websites

If you are going after 401(k) business, a defined benefit program, or any other scenario for a company and not an individual, go to the organization's competitors' websites too. Seeing what other companies are doing and how they represent themselves in the marketplace will help you understand how your contact or referral tries to differentiate itself from its competition.

If you know this, you can demonstrate that even though you aren't in the industry, you're a strategic thinker. You might want to pick out something to mention or ask about the competition, such as an acquisition, which perhaps is indicative that they have a lot of cash or that the industry is consolidating. Again, this is a great way to demonstrate to your target audience that you are different from the 90 percent of advisors who want the company's business but invest only minimal effort in learning about it and its industry.

Investigating all of these sources has two huge benefits. First, you will make a better impression on your referral than the 90 percent of advisors who take shortcuts, do not invest this kind of time, and are unprepared. Second, your contact will undoubtedly hear about the great impression you made and will appreciate the effort you made. Third, you will strengthen your relationship with both of them and become highly referable, and the "right" type of inbound referral calls will come to you from exactly the kind of people you want to continue to work with. That's the payoff for the time, effort, and hard work the homework takes.

WHAT TO DO IF YOU DON'T
FIND ENOUGH INFORMATION

Sometimes, though not often, people use all the sources just described without finding the information they need. If that happens to you, get outside the box. Challenge yourself! Don't accept defeat. Put yourself into the mindset that there must be *someone* out there who has this information, and that you can find that person or those people. Push yourself past where others would have given up.

If you try a little harder, you may just open doors you never even imagined before you found them.

Cheri, an advisor who works for an independent, had identified an organization that interested her, a home for displaced juveniles near Kalamazoo, Michigan. This organization had been around for 30 years, but it did not have a website. After exhausting her network of contacts, Cherie could not identify a single client who could help her get either access to information or in the door. She had reached what seemed to be a dead end—wherever she looked, she couldn't find any information on this organization.

Together, we probed and brainstormed to find ways she hadn't thought of that would get her out of this impasse. She could:

- Cold call the organization to find the right person and attempt to get an appointment.
- Search the Registry of Nonprofits and perhaps get the names and titles of the management team. Once Cheri had the names, she could work back through her referral network to see if anyone recognized one of them.
- Contact the local chamber of commerce to see if the organization is a member and look for employees' names.

Cheri was pretty sure that people she knew who worked and lived in the Kalamazoo area would be able to help her in her quest. She decided that using the chamber of commerce made the most sense. Cheri made an inquiry and found that the company was a member and that some employees were listed. Cheri had to peel the onion a little bit, but, lo and behold, she got a warm introduction through someone on her C list.

The point is that even if you don't know anyone in an organization, you'll be amazed at what you can come up with once you try. You may not have a single name you recognize when you start looking, but if you put in the effort, the results will follow.

DUE DILIGENCE PREPARATION QUESTIONS

Regardless of what source you use to gather this critical information, there are several questions you need to have answers to before you can have a meaningful conversation with a referral.

Here are some questions that you can ask your client or contact to help you prepare for your conversation with a referral. After your contact or client has given you the referral's contact information and you are wrapping up the conversation is the best time to ask.

I am not suggesting or advocating that you ask *all* the questions listed here—the last thing you want to do is annoy your contact or make him feel that he is being interrogated. Pick two or three of the questions based on your relationship and let the conversation flow from there. Your contact or client may provide so much information that one or two questions will give you all you need. You want to gain what I call "course knowledge"—the term used in golf for when someone advises you on how and where to hit a ball, which will ultimately save you strokes and make things easier for you.

On an Individual

How well do you know _____?

What does _____ do for a living?

What are _____'s interests outside of work?

How would you recommend I approach _____?

What do you think I need to do to earn _____'s trust and confidence?

Do you know of any things I should stay away from?

If you were me, how would you approach _____?

How long has _____ been retired?

Where did _____ work?

When did _____ sell his company?

Are there any life-changing events I should know about (such as divorce, widowed, inheritance, or settlement)?

Law Firms, CPA Firms, or Family Offices

What do you know about this organization?

Do you know anything about its decision-making process?

What do you think are its "hot buttons"?

Do you know whom it is currently using to invest its money?

What do you think I need to do to earn its trust and its business?

The answers to these questions will enable you to find out as much as you can about a person or organization, just as Kristin did. By asking a few probing questions, she found the right way to appeal to Stephanie, and you will too if you follow the same steps.

Getting the outcome you want in that first conversation is a reflection on how well you manage it. You might be having what you think is a successful conversation, but inevitably the referral is going to ask one of these questions:

- What do you know about me or our organization (non-profit)?
- Do you know what I do?
- Do you know what's going on with our family?
- Do you understand what we do here?

If you say, "I do not know much," or try to bluff your way through, you will in all likelihood have destroyed your chances of success with this referral. You will lose all credibility with this person. More important, you will probably have burned this contact not just for this opportunity, but for future ones, too.

In addition, when your name comes up in future conversations, this person will be unlikely to volunteer positive thoughts about you. You never know which connection will be the one to steer you toward your next opportunity. You cannot afford to blow it by being unprepared. Be a Kristin who was prepared and not a Sam who tried to wing it when you call or meet a referral for the first time. When you do that, the chances for success will be heavily weighted in your favor.

5

Speaking with Referrals in a Way That Tilts the Scales in Your Favor

SALMON SAYS

"You need to come across as knowledgeable, empathetic, and resourceful."

Divorcées tend to be Victor's best clients, so Victor was delighted when a mutual friend offered to introduce him to Patricia. Patricia had received a big settlement from her ex-husband and was attempting to manage her own affairs for the first time in her life.

When Victor called Patricia, he was careful to demonstrate his understanding of her situation and his sensitivity to what she was going through. He then articulated his experience with clients like her, concluding with, "That's why Heather thought it made sense for the two of us to meet. Can we schedule something now?"

They did. During the first meeting, Victor mainly asked questions and listened. At subsequent meetings, he worked on getting Patricia comfortable with the concept that she was in good hands. Only then did he simplify what Patricia thought was a daunting task: taking care of her family finances and preserving her money. After a few meetings, Patricia became a client.

When you first talk to referrals, that's where the rubber meets the road. How successful you are at getting a referral interested in what you have to say and then converting him into a client depends on how well you manage the conversation. If, like Victor, you come across as credible, knowledgeable, empathetic, and resourceful, you will make many converts. This chapter shows you exactly how Victor did this and how you can do it, too.

Your relationship with referrals is different from your relationship with clients and even contacts, so you need to use different techniques when talking with them. You have temporary credibility with referrals, but this doesn't guarantee that a referral will meet with you, become a client, or even carry on a long conversation with you. Those privileges have to be earned. Earning permanent credibility and converting it into a lasting positive impression is predicated on your conduct and your ability to ask good questions. You must demonstrate that you are interested in the referral as a person and that the relationship is not all about you. Showing your understanding of the referral's current situation and interests, and being able to clearly and confidently articulate the unique, differentiating skills that you bring to the association will go a long way toward creating a positive impression. They will set the tone for your entire relationship and allow you to fully leverage its potential.

PRE-CALL ADVICE: FOCUS MORE ON BUILDING THE RELATIONSHIP AND LESS ON THE TRANSACTION

Treat each conversation with a referral as an opportunity to develop and enhance the relationship. I have heard too many times of advisors saying something along the lines of: "Frank, this is Jack Walsh. Our mutual friend Eric suggested I give you a call. I am over here at _____, and I would love to meet you to tell you all the things we are doing here and how we can be of help to you."

When people hear something like this, most of them think, "This guy is like the all the other people who call using someone's name to get my business. All he's going to talk about is himself and what he can supposedly do for me. He has no clue about who I am, and he isn't interested in me— all he wants to do is give me his sales pitch. No way do I want to spend time on the phone with him!"

Advisors who approach referrals in this way are sending a clear message: "Let's do a transaction." Few people like being approached as transactions.

It's much more effective to think of this first communication as being like asking someone you really like out on a date. Do everything you can to make sure you don't say or do anything that might turn the person off, like acting too aggressive.

Slow down and establish a relationship before you get to business. How long that takes depends on what's going on in the referral's life and how eager she is to get started. You may invest weeks or months—perhaps even years—in the relationship (taking the referral out for meals, calling, donating to philanthropic groups that she believes in) before she is ready to do business with you.

Just remember: it's about creating relationships and expanding your network, not about doing transactions. Victor was able to establish a relationship with Patricia fairly quickly because she needed to start making decisions about her money, but Victor waited until she was ready. Only then did he take action.

BE PREPARED FOR THE WHAT-IFS

This section addresses what you should do in various situations you may encounter when you call or speak with referrals for the first time.

What If You Reach the Referral and Get the Cold Shoulder?

Sometimes you have what you thought was a great conversation with a referral, but for whatever reason, the referral doesn't respond the way you had hoped he would. Here are a few likely scenarios:

- You have left a few messages without receiving a call back from the referral.

- You spoke to the referral when he was in a rush. You were told that you would get a call back (perhaps even at a specific time), but you are still waiting for it. You feel that you have been blown off.
- You spoke to the referral and she promised to do something for you, but she hasn't done it.
- While you are speaking with the referral, your instincts tell you that things are not going well. By the end of the call, you are pretty sure that this person is not interested in what you have to say.

At this point, most people wonder whether the problem is with the referral or with them. They reflect back on the call and try to figure out where they went wrong.

My advice is, don't doubt yourself yet. The reason for the lack of response may well have nothing to do with you. The referral could be a procrastinator or someone who simply forgets to return phone calls. He could be traveling, out sick, or busy with deadlines. There are any number of things that could be going on in referrals' lives that affect their ability to focus on what you want them to do when you want them to do it.

You could go back to whoever gave you the referral, explain the situation, and see whether that person has any insight into it. You could ask her what she thinks you should do—she may then offer to call on your behalf to find out what happened.

You can then get things back on track—or, if that's not possible, at least get closure. If you did in fact do something that alienated the referral, learn from your mistake and make sure you don't repeat it. Then move on.

What If the Referral Says, "I Am All Set" or "I Am Working with Another Advisor?"

Sometimes, a referral will come right out and tell you that he is simply not interested in working with you because he's quite happy working with someone else. That may or may not be the case. Here are a few responses that can turn these people around.

> "I understand. Some of my clients have other people working with them, too. I have been told that the reasons why they work with me are . . ."

> "I understand. My clients that have substantial wealth, like you, have other people working with them as well. Candidly, no one has an exclusive on the best ideas, and working with someone else allows them to take advantage of a second opinion."

What If the Referral Says She Is Not Interested in Having a Follow-Up Meeting?

This could be because the referral was just not open to the idea of working with a new advisor, was not comfortable with the concept you suggested, or was put off by the way you asked.

Whatever the cause, after someone has said that she is not interested in a follow-up meeting, say something like,

> "I appreciate your time and that _____ connected us. I wish you well."

Or:

"I appreciate your time and that _____ connected us. I look forward to our paths crossing again, socially or professionally."

Then end the conversation.

What If the Referral Agrees to a Meeting Early in the Conversation, but You Did Not Get Through All That You Were Prepared to Say?

Once the referral agrees to meet with you, pin him down to a day and time, wrap it up, and end the conversation. Your objective for this first conversation is simply to get the referral to take a meeting with you. Do not forget that. If you continue the conversation once that has happened, you may talk him out of taking the meeting with you. Less is definitely more in situations like this, especially during your first conversation with a referral.

SPEAKING TO REFERRALS FOR THE FIRST TIME

For the initial conversation to lead to another conversation, you must do several things.

Grab the Referral's Attention with Your Connection

If your first conversation is by phone, you'll need to quickly establish why you're calling. Mention your client's or contact's name to get the referral to pay attention and listen to you. This creates temporary credibility—enough to put the referral's mind at ease and get her to listen to what you have to say. Victor did this by mentioning that Heather had suggested that he call Patricia.

Make Sure You Have the Referral's Undivided Attention

Always ask if this is a good time to talk. This is the polite thing to do, and if you don't do it, you risk talking to someone when he can't give you the time and attention you need. You may also want to ask for a specific amount of time so that the referral isn't distracted by wondering how long he's going to have to listen to you. I recommend that you ask for five minutes. Generally people will give you five minutes, especially since you are calling on the recommendation of a mutual connection.

To demonstrate how much you value and appreciate the referral's time, you must be clear and concise. Get to the point quickly, and make sure you *never* ramble on or repeat yourself. Lastly, if you gave the referral a time limit at the beginning of the call, stick to it. You should exceed it only if the referral becomes engaged in the conversation and starts asking you lots of questions.

Have a Definitive Positioning Statement and a Valid Business Reason for the Call

This shows that you understand something about the referral and the situation. Unless you have this knowledge, you shouldn't be calling.

Victor had gained his understanding of Patricia by combining information that he got from their mutual friend with his own experience and expertise. The way he demonstrated his understanding in their conversation set Patricia's mind at ease and made her receptive to a follow-up meeting with Victor.

By incorporating the information about the referral that you gathered from your contact or client, you prove that you are not one of the more than 90 percent of people who talk only about themselves.

Trigger a Reaction and Generate an Activity

At this point, the referral understands the connection, the reason for the call, and why your contact or client thought it made sense for the two of you to be connected. The next logical step in the conversation is for you to ask the referral to take a meeting with you. Victor did this when he said, "That's why Heather thought it made sense for the two of us to meet. Can we schedule something now?"

When Patricia accepted, Victor knew that he had a more permanent credibility. He also knew that he had put himself in a good position and that how he conducted himself at the follow-up meeting would determine how long that credibility lasted.

Now that you know how to stage and manage the first conversation with a referral, you're ready to review these sample scripts and, if necessary, adapt them to your style. How do you know if they need adapting? Read them out loud. If they feel and sound like you—if you can read them without feeling unnatural—they're fine for you as they are. If you find yourself stumbling over some of the words, pausing, or just feeling unnatural, they need tweaking.

If that's the case, change some of the words to incorporate your own personality into these scripts so that what you say sounds normal, natural, and not stilted. The point here is that you may change some of the wording in order to create a few scripts that you feel comfortable with and can be yourself with, and that is okay.

EXAMPLES OF TIME-TESTED
SCRIPTS THAT GET THE JOB DONE

Example 1: Speaking to a Referral for the First Time When Your Client or Contact Has Called on Your Behalf

> "Frank, hi; I am Jack Walsh. Our mutual friend Eric Day suggested I give you a call. Did he mention I was going to call you?"

Continue with:

> "Is this a good time for us to speak?"

Or:

> "Am I getting you at a good time?"

If the person says no, continue with:

> "Is there a better day and time for us to chat, as Eric wanted us to connect? Please let me know what's best for you."

If the person says yes, demonstrate your understanding of her situation from the due diligence you did. What you say here will, of course, depend upon what you know the person is looking for, so you'll need to develop your own script. Here's something that worked with someone high up at Apple:

> "I do not know how much Paul told you about me, but I am with Merrill Lynch. I am a principal on a team, with over 25 years' experience managing wealth for officers in publicly traded companies that have complex concentrated stock positions. We recently helped some of the Google guys, and when Eric and I were talking about some of the creative things we did there, he told me you were at Apple. He thought we should get to know each other."

If what you say at first is well received, continue with something like:

> "Is there a good time for you over the next two weeks to get together?"

Or:

"What's a good day and time for you?"

Or:

"Is this something we can schedule now?"

Or:

"Is this something we can schedule now, since Eric suggested we meet?"

Example 2: Speaking to a Referral for the First Time When No One Has Called on Your Behalf

This is probably going to be a bigger challenge, since the person is not expecting the call and may be skeptical. So mention your client or contact's name early in the conversation to bridge the gap and open the person's mind to hearing what you have to say.

Begin immediately with:

"Joan, hi; I am Karen Williams. You and I have not spoken before. I am calling today because Beth Miller suggested I reach out to you."

Or:

"Joan, hi; I am Karen Williams. Our mutual friend Beth Miller suggested I give you a call."

Either way, continue with:

> "Is this a good time for us to speak?"

Or:

> "Am I getting you at a good time?"

If the person says no, continue with:

> "Is there a better day and time for us to chat, as Beth wanted us to connect? Please let me know what's best for you."

If the person says yes, continue with:

> "Beth told me to send regards."

Or:

> "When was the last time you spoke to Beth?"

Or,

> "I was with Beth the other day, and she told me to give you a call.
>
> "I am with Sun Trust in the medical specialty group. I manage financial matters both for partners personally and for their practice, whether they need a loan, a 401(k), or financial planning and wealth management. Beth mentioned that you are now the partner in charge of a

10-person group, and since working with groups that
size is my bread and butter, she said we should know
each other and meet. That is the reason for my call today.
I would love to get to know you better, since we run in
the same circles, and of course because Beth brought us
together and said we should."

Continue with:

"How does that sound to you?"

Or:

"Since Beth suggested it, when would be a good day and
time for you?"

POST-CALL DEBRIEFING

After the call, ask yourself how well it went. That will be
easy if you have paid attention to the referral's responses
during the call. If the referral asked questions and displayed
enthusiasm (through his words or inflections), you had his
attention and interest. If the conversation took place in
person, the referral's body language should have told you how
the conversation was going. Was the referral enthusiastic,
complimentary, and focused? Did she smile a lot, use her
hands to make a point, and speak with inflections? Was
she leaning forward or talking in an animated way when
describing her situation? If you can say yes to most, if not all,

of these questions, chances are that the referral was looking forward to taking the conversation to the next phase.

If, on the other hand, the referral was checking his smartphone, shuffling papers around, or getting up during the conversation, or if he said he had to cut the conversation short, he was probably not truly interested in what you had to say. If someone looked at his watch, chances are he was bored. If he was hesitant or guarded with his answers, chances are he was uncomfortable. Someone who responds this way at first will be harder to turn around than someone who was more positive at first, but if he agrees to meet with you or speak with you again, you may well be able to do it.

THE REFERRAL AGREED
TO A MEETING—WHAT NEXT?

At the first meeting, continue the process of developing a meaningful and long-lasting relationship. You do this by following this sequence of steps:

- *Gathering information.* First, find out how well suited the two of you are to working together. Ask good questions and listen to the answers to better understand the referral's situation and determine whether there is a fit. This will save time and determine timelines and what your chances for success will be.
- *Giving information.* Second, respond to the referral's "selling cues." Gauge the prospective client's interest in your style, the way you operate, your investment strategies,

and your solution for addressing her "hot buttons." Respond to what is truly important to the referral, and give examples of your experiences with clients that mirror the referral's current situation and align with her needs.

- *Getting a commitment.* If you have done the first two, you should now be in the enviable position of being able to convert this prospect into a client.

The gathering and giving information steps may occur during a single meeting, or they may occur over the course of several meetings. It depends on how urgently the referral needs an advisor, the amount of time allocated for the first meeting, and the meeting dynamics.

Gathering Information

Effective first meetings are shaped by your ability to ask good questions and to *listen*. Prospective clients make decisions in a series of logical and predictable steps. By asking good questions on the front end, you will:

- Reinforce your credibility by demonstrating that you care.
- Motivate and sustain your prospect's interest, stimulate his thinking, and get both of you to win-win.
- Help you understand her decision-making process.
- Gain "perfect knowledge" to determine whether this relationship is a perfect fit.
- Know where you stand.

Making a good impression means listening well. You need to let your prospective client do more talking than you do. Good advisors are good listeners. Great advisors are great listeners. A great listener knows how to ask the right questions and knows when to be quiet. Great listeners also know how to control the conversation. Ineffective listeners make mistakes, interrupt, misinterpret the client's needs, and forget things. They are too worried about saying everything they want to say to listen well.

Most people prefer talking to listening. The more you listen to your prospect, the more he will like you. The better you listen, the better you will be able to gather important information, guide the conversation, and respond effectively to the other person's needs. Remember, people like doing business with people who make them feel comfortable.

Probing for Needs

A need is a selling cue that occurs when a prospective client indicates an interest in your service or identifies a requirement that you can fulfill. Your chances of success are greatly increased when you show how you and your organization can meet the person's specific needs.

Beginning Questions

Your ability to ask intelligent, forthright questions sets the tone for the meeting and the development of the relationship. Here are some good beginning questions:

- "What's going on in your world?"
- "What's going on?"
- "What are some things you'd like me to know about you?"
- "How can I possibly help you?"

- "What predispositions do you have about _____ [our organization]?"
- "Are you working with an advisor now?"
- "Who else are you speaking with?"
- "What other firms are you speaking to?"
- "Where are you with them in the process?"
- "What is your timeline for selling the company?"
- "What is your timeline for selecting a wealth management firm?"

You may need to ask only one or two of these questions because you will learn all you need to know from the referral's answers. Regardless, after you ask any or all of these questions, stop talking and listen—let the referral tell you exactly what you need to know.

Attitude Questions

You need to get the referral to open up and let you know how she feels about things.

These questions are used to identify the prospective client's personal needs, values, attitude, and sense of urgency concerning her needs. Knowing how your clients feel about these things will help you better understand what the real issues are. Here are some useful attitude questions:

- "What's important to you when evaluating wealth management firms?"
- "What do you like or not like about what you have heard from the others?"
- "In your opinion, what is the perfect relationship with an advisor?"

- "Can you describe your ideal relationship with an advisor?"
- "What would you like to know about me?"
- "How would you determine our success in working with you?"

Victor and Patricia's meeting was scheduled for 60 minutes. For the first 15 minutes, they just chatted about Patricia's current personal situation and what it felt like not being with her husband after so many years. During this time, Victor got a sense of Patricia's concerns, fears, and discomfort. He asked several questions, but what really got Patricia to open up was the best opening question of all:

"What's going on?"

With this simple question, Victor learned that Patricia felt overwhelmed by dealing with the family's finances on a day-to-day basis because her ex-husband had once taken care of these matters. She also admitted to feeling embarrassed at needing help in this area and wanting to work with someone who would simplify things for her. Victor's ability to ask the right question at the right time got Patricia to open up about all that.

Commitment Questions

These questions enable you to see where you stand and what you should do next: continue to strengthen the relationship, do business, or ask more questions. They bring you closer to closure or to an activity that moves the process forward (agree, decide, plan, commit, recommend, provide). You should use these questions at the end of the meeting as you are wrapping up. Here are some commitment questions you should use:

- "When we meet again, will you be able to provide me with your financial statements?"
- "Will you be recommending us to _____?"
- "Should we plan on having you come to the office to meet the rest of the team?"
- "When can we get back together so that I can respond in more detail to the questions you raised?"

When Victor first met with Patricia, he came by himself; that made the most sense because bringing in other members of the team might have seemed too heavy-handed—even intimidating. You should always ask yourself whether it's most appropriate for you to go alone or to bring team members.

The meeting went well, and Victor was able to schedule their follow-up meeting right there. The reason things went well was that Victor was in control, was organized, asked good questions in the proper order, provided a little insight into what he does and how he does it, and related that to Patricia's situation. This gave Patricia a feeling that Victor truly did understand what she was going through, so she was willing to let him set up a follow-up meeting.

Another advisor, Jody, had a meeting with Gloria, the matriarch of a family whose name is on a sports stadium. This was supposedly an exploratory, get-to-know-each-other meeting. When Jody explained the situation, it sounded very much like Victor's opportunity with Patricia.

However, Jody handled the first meeting very differently. Jody didn't go alone; she brought Sandy, her partner, and she also brought a slick, 30-page "pitch book" detailing all the great things their organization could do. Instead of asking Gloria questions and listening to her answers, Jody and Sandy spent the lunch talking about themselves, their organization, and what they could do for Gloria.

Needless to say, Gloria declined to meet with the two women again—or even speak with them on the telephone. When you have a first meeting with a client, leave the pitch book at the office and make sure you do more asking and listening than talking. You need to understand what is important to your prospective client before you attempt to provide any information about yourself.

Giving Information

Once you have enough information about your prospective client and/or his organization, let him know what you and your organization can do for him. What's important here is that your response is focused on the prospect's needs. Victor's firm could have offered to do many things for Patricia, such as give her investment opportunities that are generally open only to institutional clients but were also open to her because of the amount of her assets. But to Victor's credit, he did not do that. He stayed on task and continued to offer only the experience and expertise his group had with other divorcées as a differentiator. By responding only to your prospect's specific needs, you will be able to demonstrate that:

- You listened and understood.
- Your organization will provide the best solutions.
- Your prospect will feel comfortable working with you and your organization.
- You solved your prospect's problem.
- You deserve the business.

If you can do all this, 9 times out of 10 you will get the business because you've proven that there is a fit between you and your organization's capabilities and the prospective client's perception of what's important to him (the need). Your solution is better, and it's unique.

If your prospective client is a nonprofit, an attorney, a CPA, or anyone who reports to someone else, this is also your opportunity to show that you and your firm will not only meet the client's needs, but also make her look good in the process.

Features, Benefits, and Proof Sources

When responding and giving information, I have found that the majority of advisors talk about features. That is, they talk about themselves, their team, their investment philosophy, and how wonderful it is to work with them.

Conceptually that is a good start, but prospective clients want more. They want to know how they will benefit—and the best advisors not only tell them what those benefits are but personalize the benefits and make it easy for the prospective clients to visualize them. So when you are educating your prospective clients on why they should consider you as an advisor, incorporate these three ingredients:

- *Features.* What are your solutions or distinguishing characteristics? Victor's were his and his team's years of experience working with divorcées, their sensitivity, their understanding of Patricia's feelings and situation, the platform they use for divorcées who do not want to take risks, and the fact that they had a team that was deep enough to do all the things that Patricia needed help with, such as paying bills, estate planning, and so on. To see the full list of all the features Victor's team offered, see Table 5-1. Going through this exercise will enable you to flush out all the things you can offer your prospective clients. As you start to develop your strategy and approach, it will help you prepare a cogent response to your prospective client's needs.

- *Benefits.* What are the benefits of those features to the prospective client? What will you and your team actually do for her? For Patricia, the benefits were all about making her life easier, preserving her money, and giving her peace of mind. The message that Victor and his team sent to Patricia was that she was not alone, that they empathized with her, and that with their support, she could manage things going forward. Their approach made her feel empowered and feel that with them, she would have the same comfort and freedom from worry about finances that she'd had when her husband was managing them.

- *Proof source.* Show the prospective client real-life examples of how you and your organization have done similar things before and how well they worked. Victor did this at the third meeting by having Patricia meet his team. They shared a few stories of other divorcée clients who

Table 5-1   Features, Benefits, and Proof Sources

Area	Feature	Benefit	Proof Source
People	Knowledgeable, on call	Anyone the client speaks to can handle the call	Meet the team
	Client-driven, limited number of accounts	Lots of attention, become very involved holistically	
	Ask lots of questions— good listeners	Know what is important to client, proactive with ideas	
	Smart		Meet the team
	Pay attention to details	Will not have any surprises and will have peace of mind	Examples
	Dig deep	Uncover things most firms don't	Case study
Delivery	Open architecture	Not limited to a single organization's offerings— greater risk reduction	Meet the experts
	Customized solutions	Will outperform a canned approach on five-year track record	Documents
	Our process of customization	Reflects intimate knowledge— not cookie-cutter	Case study

Delivery	Platform and products fully integrated	Emphasizes what you as the client want to accomplish	White paper
Organization	Global institution	Access to resources that are typically reserved for institutional clients	Office visit— NYC?
		Additional support with expertise from all over the world	Office visit
	Boutique shop	Feels like a small family office with big organization support	Office visit
Expertise	Estate planning	Wealth transfer done right, giving client peace of mind	Case study
	Tax management		Case study
	Concentrated stock management		White paper
	Banking and lending		Case study
	Asset management		
	Mergers and acquisitions		
	Private equity		

had had the same worries. They showed her examples of asset allocation and monthly statements, including the bill management services. Here again, they stressed the benefits with a visual that made it easier for Patricia to understand and get comfortable with what these services had given other divorcées—the services made their lives easier and gave them peace of mind. More than likely this is what put Victor's presentation over the top and helped Patricia visualize herself as a client.

Table 5-1 gives an example of the features, benefits, and proof sources exercise that Victor used to separate himself from the competition when he was going after this $15 million opportunity with Patricia.

Getting a Commitment

How a prospective client responds to your attempts to get a commitment will tell you a lot about your chances of doing business with him. Sometimes people send signals that they are ready to move forward and/or commit. And sometimes you have to ask to find out where you stand. Here are some of the most important clues.

Buying/Commitment Signals

A buying or commitment signal is a clear message from the prospective client indicating that she is ready to move forward. These clues are not difficult to spot. They are always phrased in the form of a question or statement about implementation. The prospective client has moved from "whether" to asking things like:

- "How long would it take for you to gear up to take over my account?"
- "What do we need to do to get started?"
- "When can you sit and meet with my estate attorney and/or CPA?"
- "Can you send me the paperwork?"
- "Can I speak to a few of your references?"

When clients ask questions like this, they just want to be told how to go about getting started with you. That is why these kinds of questions are called commitment signals—and why it's so important that you respond to them right away. You have developed momentum and the opportunity to close. The opportunity is now, and you need to seize it. If you put it off, you run the risk of losing that momentum and your prospective client's willingness to move forward with you. My experience is that time kills all deals. When you reach this point, don't wait, and don't procrastinate—go for it.

Closing

This is the logical conclusion to a well-orchestrated strategy. It's time to ask for the order. You've earned the privilege of asking for that by what you've done so far: demonstrated that you understand the client, that you are the best solution, and that this is the logical end of a natural progression. Studies by *Sales & Marketing Management* magazine show that 62 percent of people responsible for sales never ask for the order—and thus never get it.

You should always be closing in every meeting you have with a prospective client. Every conversation or meeting should lead to some sort of follow-up, with a commitment being made between you and the prospective client. Every commitment made increases your bond and enhances your comfort with each other. By the time you ask for the order, you will have developed an excellent rapport that makes it easy for you to ask for it.

When you do, remember and recap: the client's need, her "buy-in" on your solution, and any prior commitments she made to you. After you go through that review, here's how to ask for the business:

> "You said that if we could demonstrate that we could improve your portfolio's performance, you would recommend us. Are you prepared to do that now?"

> "You said you needed a global organization that has top-flight research and access to the best money managers, both proprietary and nonproprietary. Have you found anyone out there that would be a better solution than we would?"

> "You have now evaluated several organizations. Do you feel that our team meets your needs and is the best fit for you?"

> "What more do you need in order to get comfortable with me and _____?"

> "What more do you need to know in order for you to get comfortable working with me?"

"What more do I need to do in order for you to get comfortable with me?"

"What more do we need to do in order to move forward and begin working together?"

"What more do we need to do to get you comfortable with us and to move forward and begin working together?"

When Patricia met the team, Victor sensed that she was visualizing herself as a client when she said, "Do you have a minimum to get started with you in order for the team to start taking care of all my bills?"

They gave her an exact amount, and she seemed pleased, so Victor sensed (rightly) that it was time to ask for the business. When he said,

"What more do we need to do to get you comfortable with us and to move forward and begin working together?" Patricia smiled and said,

"Nothing else. This is a big decision, and I need to think about it a little more. I will get back to you within the next two weeks."

Within one week, Victor got the call from Patricia, and she is now an $18 million client. Jody and Sandy are still trying to schedule that second meeting with Gloria. Victor was successful because he asked good questions, listened well, responded properly, managed expectations, brought in the right people at the right time, described the features, constantly demonstrated the value of these features (the benefits) to Patricia, and made it easy for Patricia to visualize those benefits. By the time Patricia was ready to select an

advisory team, Victor and his team had distinguished themselves and had earned the right to ask for the business.

Not enough advisors have the confidence, temerity, and
ability to actually ask for the business. But if you follow the
advice given here, you will have more success getting referrals
to *yes*, becoming a client. Victor did a great job of managing
the process. If you do the things Victor did, the scales will tilt
in your favor, too.

6

Making Centers of Influence Better Referral Sources

SALMON SAYS
"CPAs crunch numbers; lawyers focus on legal matters. Whether they admit it or not, they all need to make rain."

Thomas, an advisor on the Gulf Coast of Florida, wanted top estate attorneys and CPAs to become an integral part of his strategy of bringing in new clients with more than $25 million each in assets. He set up initial meetings with three estate attorneys and three CPAs and brought value to each meeting. He brought in experts to discuss particular subject matter, conducted training programs that provided credit, held seminars for clients and prospects, introduced the attorneys and CPAs to his CEO to get his reading on the markets, and got together with each of them every other month for lunch. Over time, Thomas established credibility. Still, even with all this effort, after a year, Thomas hadn't seen any *results. But he maintained his "drip" campaign anyway. After 18 months, introductions to exactly the kind of people he wanted to meet started coming his way. Six months later, one of those people became a client—and over the months and years, others did, too.*

Most advisors are told by their managers that the best referrals come from attorneys and CPAs (centers of influence, or COIs). They do—but, as Thomas found, getting these referrals takes time. You may woo a COI for months or even years before he gives you a referral. Not every advisor has the patience to wait that long—or enough ideas, reasons, or items of value to justify repeated meetings with and calls to the same COI. In this chapter, you will see how Thomas kept his relationships with these people growing, step by step, and how he parlayed those relationships into ongoing referrals.

A warning: even if you follow a similar strategy, you may not get the same results. Even after a relationship is established, many advisors find that COIs are not as forthcoming with introductions as they could be. Many advisors lose patience and abandon the COI referral plan.

However, these people can provide countless untapped opportunities—if you can come up with a game plan that is right for you. You can't just meet a COI and then wait, expecting her to provide you with countless unsolicited referrals. You need to drive the process and set expectations by having a plan, a clear road map; otherwise it will not happen.

That's what Len, one of the principals with a Barron's top 100 team in Boston, did about his firm's one-sided relationship with estate attorneys. He embarked on a plan to correct that imbalance that was easy to follow. His plan is detailed in this chapter to help you create yours when you are faced with similar challenges.

Here is how Thomas and Len got started.

IDENTIFYING POTENTIAL COIs
YOU MAY WANT TO WORK WITH

- *Create a list of your top A and B clients.* Most, if not all, of your clients have existing relationships with at least one CPA and perhaps several attorneys. So first, put together a list of your top A and B clients. Thomas came up with 25 names from Tampa to Naples; Len had 50. The exact number you come up with will depend on the number of years you have been in the business, the number of clients you currently have or want to have, and the relationships you have with your clients. The important thing here is to make the time, put the list together, and get started.

- *Contact each of these clients.* Begin to reach out to these people, even if you already have contact information for their COIs. Whether you have the information or not, reach out to your clients. If you don't have the contact information, ask for it; if you already have it, confirm it. Do this by phone, not by e-mail—in an e-mail, it's too hard for you to articulate why you want the contact information and too easy for clients to delay responding to your request.

Once you have the client on the phone, say something like:

"I'm touching base with you today because I am updating your records about the professionals you are using. Do you have a minute?"

Here are a few ways you may want to continue:

"Are you still working with _____?"

"Who is preparing your taxes?"

"Do you like _____?"

"Do you have an estate attorney?"

You can conclude this part of the conversation in one of two ways.

If you have never made contact with the client's COI before, say:

"Would you mind if I called _____ to let him know that we work together?"

If you have made contact with the COI before, say:

"Would you mind if I called _____ again to get reacquainted?"

Thomas and Len both got 100 percent cooperation from their clients. You probably will receive the information you are looking for, too, if you follow the script.

- *Prepare a list of the COIs your clients use.* Once you've talked to your clients, make a list of COI names and contact information. Take a look to see if there are any trends. For example, some names may jump out at you because these COIs are working with more than one of your clients. These are the COIs you should contact first. Next, see which of these COIs have great reputations. Thomas identified eight estate attorneys and four CPAs who were working with more than one of his clients and had great reputations. Many of Len's clients worked with the same six estate attorneys in greater Boston, attorneys who were among the best in the area. Thomas and Len leveraged their clients' relationships with these people to open doors and develop their own relationships with these COIs and their firms.

CALLING TO GET THE COI TO TAKE A FIRST MEETING WITH YOU

Too often, advisors reach a COI and immediately go into sales pitch mode. That is not going to work. COIs get solicited all the time, and the only way to separate yourself from the pack is to slow down and take a more holistic approach.

The purpose of your first call is to get the COI to take a meeting with you. If your client has not called on your behalf, you should consider saying something along the lines of:

"Hello, _____. This is _____. I am at _____, and I have been working with _____, who is a client we have in common. I am reaching out to you today because I was speaking to _____ the other day and your name came up, and I realized we have never met."

Continue with:

"Am I getting you at a good time?"

If the COI says yes, continue with:

"I think it is important that we get together so that I can understand your practice better. Can we schedule something now for me to come to your office for a 30-minute meeting? Please let me know over the next two weeks what's the best day and time for you."

If your contact or client has called ahead on your behalf, begin with something like:

"_____, this is _____. I am calling you because _____ told me that he called you on my behalf and suggested that I contact you directly."

Continue with:

"Is this a good time for us to speak?"

If the COI says yes, continue with:

"I don't know how much _____ told you about me. I am with _____. Are you familiar with us? We work predominantly with _____, _____, and

_____ [whatever your profile is], and _____ mentioned that your practice also specializes in this area."

Or, you can say:

> "I don't know how much _____ told you about me. I am with _____. It is a policy of my practice to know other professional advisors that my clients are using. I understand that your specialty is _____ [fill in the blank; some examples may be estate planning or trust service]. This is our specialty, too."

Either way, continue with:

> "_____ thought it would be mutually beneficial if we met. I would welcome the opportunity to spend some time with you, giving us a chance to know each other a little better and allowing me to understand your practice better. Can I come to your office for a 20- to 30-minute meeting with you next week? I have time at _____ and _____."

Or:

> "What day and time is better for you?"

If you use this approach, chances are that you will get the meeting. The COI will take that first meeting with you mainly because you have a mutual client. It makes sense for the two of you to be on the same page—you can probably help each other to serve that client.

Some COIs may take the meeting because they don't know the extent and strength of your relationship with this mutual client, and they are not going to risk their relationship with the client by saying no to you.

MAKING THE FIRST MEETING ABOUT DEVELOPING THE RELATIONSHIP

Keep the first meeting brief, and keep it all about the COI. The major objectives of the first meeting are to make a favorable impression by asking good questions and being a good listener, and to get a second meeting scheduled.

Again, think of this first meeting as a first date with someone you like. You want to make a good first impression so that you have a shot at a second date. The format, strategy, and types of questions to use here are the same as those in Chapter 5. Some of the questions you should be asking during the first meeting are:

- "Tell me about yourself."
- "What is your area of expertise?"
- "What is the firm's area of specialization?"
- "Do you currently work with any other advisors?"
- "If so, with whom?"
- "Are you happy?"
- "What do you look for in a 'formal' relationship with an advisor?"
- "What other things are important to you?"
- "Do you like to do educational programs for clients?"

- "What would we need to do in order for you to get comfortable with us as a potential resource?"

The answers to these questions will tell you what the COI's expectations are. If the COI asks about you, it is mission-critical that you articulate your value proposition clearly and succinctly. So before the meeting, make sure you have a simple, brief, and compelling description of the benefits of your practice.

You want to be able to demonstrate something quantifiable, something that shows the value of what you and your organization can do with and for the COI and his firm. How clear and compelling your presentation is will determine whether or not the COI starts to envision your value to him and his firm. Think in terms of giving the kind of information described in Chapter 5. Remember: the COI needs to know what you will bring to the table. Is it contacts, knowledge, resources, or understanding of a certain investment strategy that would be beneficial to his clients?

Somehow, you must distinguish yourself from the others. Thomas offered COIs educational forums on topical subjects that resonated with their clients. His organization provided programs that allowed them to get the CE credit they needed. Thomas also talked about his firm's support for local philanthropic causes and how it provided estate and tax expertise in areas where its clients had complex needs. He did much of this over gourmet lunches, which Thomas was willing to underwrite.

Len had a more direct approach. His firm was known in the area as the premier wealth management team for executives in publicly traded companies with concentrated stock positions. Len wanted to meet estate attorneys who worked with companies that were about to go public, as he knew that when the company did go public, its executives would have an immediate need for financial advisors. With an attorney on his side, he'd be well positioned to get referrals and meet that need.

DEVELOPING THE OPPORTUNITY

If the first meeting goes well, you may have an opportunity to move the relationship along. Giving the COIs a consistent experience of goodwill and demonstrating value over time with actions, not just with words, is what will do that.

Thomas proved his goodwill and his value by coming back for monthly scheduled meetings with the COIs. Some of the meetings included, but were not limited to, introductions to other members of Thomas's organization, including the CEO, vice chairmen, head of client relationships, and VP of trust and estate services. Thomas also conducted the seminars and, of course, attended those nice lunches at some of the best restaurants in the area.

Len proved his value by introducing estate attorneys to some of his clients. Whatever it is that you commit to, deliver on time and deliver consistently. COIs get requests from your colleagues in the business all the time. You need to be consistent in your execution of whatever it is that has been mutually agreed to in the previous steps.

Remember, it took Thomas 18 months to get a referral—but he now averages two introductions per year from 6 of the 12 COI relationships that he developed during that time. Those same 12 relationships have led to at least three new clients per year at an average of $25 million in net new assets per new relationship, totaling $75 million in net new assets each year purely from this strategy.

Do not compare yourself to Thomas when it comes to the number of new clients and the amount of net new assets you bring in. What matters is what you bring to the table and the consistency and professionalism you display with your actions.

Equity in a COI relationship is about trust, and it takes time to build that. COIs will make introductions for you only when they have full confidence in you. This confidence is the essence of trust, and it is a prerequisite for any ongoing referral relationship. Remember, this is a marathon, not a sprint. Typically, it takes at least a year to solidify the relationship and start receiving referrals from these professionals the way Thomas did.

PIVOTING WHEN THE RELATIONSHIP IS TOO ONE-SIDED—SALMON'S MUTUALLY BENEFICIAL LEAD EXCHANGE PROCESS WITH COIS

Many advisors get frustrated when they work with COIs because they feel as if the relationship is out of balance. Advisors give out numerous referrals and don't receive many (or any!) in return. And, when they press the COI, they often hear things like:

- "I do not know of any situations now where there is a need."
- "None of my clients are in the market for a new advisor. If something comes up, I will let you know."
- "I am not comfortable recommending any advisors. If anything goes wrong, it would not reflect well on me, and I don't want to risk losing any clients."
- "I am not comfortable recommending any advisors. I need to remain objective, and I can't recommend one person over another."

Many advisors don't have the patience to woo a COI for 6, 12, or even 18 months without getting a referral. Other advisors give up because they do not know where to take the conversation next. If either of these sounds like you, you're not alone. Len felt the same way until we figured out ways for him to take the initiative and keep moving the relationships forward. You need to do this, too, and give the relationships the time and effort they need if they are to grow. And as you will see from what Len did, grow they will—if you stick to a plan like his!

Start by admitting that you can't be all things to all people. If you've been trying for a while and are starting to feel discouraged, it makes sense for you to narrow your focus and identify a select group of CPAs and attorneys. It is unrealistic to expect a referral from most of the COIs on your long list. To narrow it, ask yourself these critical questions:

- Do I like this person?
- Do I get along with him?
- Is she a good person?
- Is he competent?
- Do I trust her?

After you have reflected on those questions, you are ready to proceed.

NARROWING THE NUMBER OF YOUR COI RELATIONSHIPS

After not receiving any referrals over an 18-month period, Len went through his long list, asked those questions, and concluded that of the six estate attorneys he had been speaking and meeting with, he could say yes on all counts for only three of them. You may reach a similar conclusion after 12 months or after 24 months, but give the process at least a year before you begin narrowing your COI relationships. When you do begin to narrow the list, consider the number of referrals you have made to each and what kind of reciprocity you expected by a certain time. Go through your long list— can you find three or four CPAs and/or attorneys who have your confidence? Write down their information.

In Chapter 8, you will find a sample sales pipeline for contacts; you can add these COIs to it to make sure that you stay organized and focused on developing and nurturing these relationships and moving the opportunities forward.

CALLING THOSE COIs TO SEE IF THEY ARE INTERESTED IN A MORE FORMAL REFERRAL LEAD EXCHANGE

Here is where you start to flush out how sincere a COI is about developing a mutually beneficial referral exchange with you. Again, the only way this is going to happen is if you initiate the conversation effectively and guide it efficiently. After you get through the small talk, say something along the lines of,

> "I was thinking about you and was curious: are you still in growth mode?"

How many people will say no to that question? If the COI says yes, you are off to a good start. To take the relationship to the next level, continue by saying something like,

> "Great. So are we. I was thinking of a way we may be able to introduce each other to clients or other people that meet our respective profiles. Would you be up for meeting for a half hour over breakfast to discuss this?"

Again, chances are that the COI will say yes. If she does, continue with,

> "What day over the next few weeks works best for you?"

If she names a day, you are off to the races. In Len's case, all three attorneys said they were interested, and the follow-up meal was scheduled. Breakfast works well because it does not interfere with your nine-to-five revenue-producing hours. Keeping the first meeting to 30 minutes demonstrates that the meeting has a specific, mutually agreed-upon purpose—by sticking to the stated time limit, you show that you respect and value the COI's time and that you keep your commitments.

WHAT TO DO AND SAY AT THE MEETING

Go through the pleasantries, remind the COI that you promise that the meeting will take only 30 minutes, and, as you get down to business, broach the subject of a lead exchange by saying:

> "I am glad we were able to get together today. I've enjoyed our association, and I think we can continue to work together and make introductions on each other's behalf. Are you still open to this idea (or concept)?"

Chances are that the COI will say yes—after all, that was the reason for the get-together! So continue with:

> "You know, I was thinking that over the next 12 months, I am pretty sure that I can introduce you to people who meet your profile. What would you expect in terms of the number of introductions you'd like me to make on your behalf over the next year?"

He will give you a number. As long as the number is reasonable, say,

"That's fair. In reverse, what should I expect in terms of the number of introductions you can make on my behalf?"

Chances are that the COI will give you the same number he gave for himself. If he does not, say that you think the same number of introductions would be fair, or propose a reasonable number that's close to the one he gave for himself. Whatever you do, don't propose an unreasonable number—you won't like what happens if you do that!

Once you have agreed on numbers, things can go awry. Past experience shows that even when both people have good intentions, their mutually agreed-to idea can come to nothing. So it's important to say something like,

"My experience is that most of these alliances don't work out as planned. I want to make sure that doesn't happen to us. So I suggest that we meet *formally* once per quarter—maybe for breakfast like this, maybe after work—to see how we are doing. Now, I am sure we will be speaking periodically in between discussing opportunities, but this way we can keep things going and make sure we are staying on track. How does that sound to you?"

Even if the COI agrees to this, you are still not done. Lawyers are focused on their practices. CPAs are focused on number crunching. Client development is a tertiary activity to them—but to you, it's a crucial component of your business. Most COIs need coaching from you as to how this referral-networking concept needs to work. Bring up some of the perceived or implied objections COIs normally have to these arrangements by continuing with:

> "Great. Now that we have a good understanding of how we are going to work together, I'd like to share a few things with you. As you may or may not know, my client profile is [describe the type of people that are in your book of business here]. You may have a client who's looking for an advisor immediately—say, after a 911 or a liquidity event. Meeting people like that gives me a lightning in a bottle opportunity, but these events may never occur. So it's more important that you know what kind of clients I'd most like to work with. If you know people who fit this profile, and if you would be comfortable introducing me to them—just so that they are aware of me as a resource—that would be great. That's what I will do for you. When I introduce you to my clients, like you, I need to maintain objectivity, and I may introduce them to someone else, too. In the end, they will make the choice as to whom they want to work with. Obviously I will put in a good word for you. Like you, I just want to meet more people that fit my profile through a warm introduction from people I know— just so that they are aware of me as a resource. Does this make sense to you?"

Always end with a question like this so that you can find out how receptive to the arrangement the COI really is. And if she is still on board, close with,

"When do you want to get started?"

Len used that process in sequential order, following the scripts verbatim and meeting me for monthly coaching sessions. Then he missed a month. When we next saw each other, I said,

"Len, I really do not like missing our scheduled sessions. I feel like we are making progress, and I don't want to lose our momentum."

He told me not to worry, that it was okay. Well, I've heard that before, and usually it is not good. So I said,

"Len, you say it is okay—why is it okay?"

With his biggest smile, he said,

"I've been busy—I picked up four $10 million clients through COIs!"

When I asked how, he said,

"It was very simple. I followed our outlined plan, followed the scripts, and asked."

I said, "It's that simple."

He said, "Yes, it was. It is amazing what happens when you ask the right way."

So what can you do with a plan like this? Imagine that you have established, say, three strong CPA relationships and three strong lawyer relationships, and they each suggest four new relationships per year. That's 24 warm introductions made on your behalf. How many of those 24 do you think you can convert to clients? At least 3 or 4? Would you be happy with that? If so, follow this plan. Many of your colleagues around the country have, and they are enjoying success like Len's.

TRACKING MECHANISM USED TO ENSURE THAT YOU GET FAVORABLE ROI FROM YOUR FORMAL COI RELATIONSHIPS

Many formal alliances begin well, but unless there is accountability, little will result from them. To get the results you want, create a scorecard like the one in Table 6-1 and check it at least monthly. This will keep you focused and hold you accountable to your commitments. This scorecard is for your use only. It should never be shared with the COI

Table 6-1   COI Relationship Scorecard

	Number of Names or Introductions per Quarter or per Year	Number of Referral Meetings per Quarter	Number of New Clients per Year
COI			
Committed			
Actual			

(although you can certainly remind him what he committed to when and what has actually happened).

Here is an explanation of the fields:

COI. The name of the COI with whom you have a formal alliance. This makes it easy to see who has committed to what and how each is doing with your plan.

Number of names and introductions per quarter or per year. Place the number of names or introductions the COI has committed to, either by quarter or by year, here. "Committed" means the number of names the COI promised to provide. "Actual" means the number of names you have received to date. This way, when you get together at your quarterly meetings, you will see the differences (if any!) in black and white and know how you are doing.

Number of referral meetings per quarter. This is your estimate. You should base it on the experience you have had when other people have given you referrals. For example, if a COI says that he can make six introductions for you and/or give you six names, and you think you will get a 50 percent hit rate, the number in that box would be three. Now, I realize that the percentage will vary based on the strength of the relationship and/or other factors. I used 50 percent based on the experience I've had coaching many advisors at different levels, and I think it is a realistic expectation when the referral comes from a COI.

Number of new clients per year. Again, you estimate this, based on your experience with warm introductions. If you think your hit rate will be 33 percent, the number in that box would be one. Again, I realize that it is based on the strength of the relationship and/or other factors. However, 33 percent is what I have seen to be the average.

Remember, if you have four formal COI alliances, and you are meeting 24 new prospects each year and bringing in 4 of them as new clients, you still have up to 20 referral relationships to cultivate. Probably some or all of these 20 will eventually become clients or turn out to be excellent referral sources for you.

If you follow the ideas outlined in this chapter, chances are that you will find that the number of referrals you receive from COIs will increase. Realistically, you can't expect 100 percent of these referrals to become clients, but some of them will (usually a good 25 percent), and the others will go into your pipeline. These new clients and the greater access to people who meet your profile that the process provides are a pretty good return on your investment of time.

7

Thriving in Changing Times

SALMON SAYS

"What separates the players from the fakers is the ability to exceed expectations in tough times."

In 2008, when many advisors were running scared and saw their clients' portfolios decrease in value by as much as 50 percent, Eric, an advisor with one of the nation's leading regional banks, had a record year. How did he do it? Where others saw disaster, he saw opportunity. Eric took a proactive approach with his clients and kept working on new ideas. His clients' portfolios were down, but not as much as many others'. His clients appreciated his input, visibility, and hard work. Eric attributes his growth to "a few things. First and foremost, you must recognize that now it is not about performance, it is all about relationships. I have a detailed plan as to when and how often I stay in touch with my top clients. Second, when my clients praise me, I pick my spots and ask for

referrals the way you taught me. Third, when I have been calling
these potential clients, now more than ever they are willing to
listen to a new voice. Candidly, there is no better time to be an
advisor in this business, and I am going to help as many people
as I can."

In these tough economic times, managers are constantly
telling advisors to be proactive and stay in touch with their
clients. That's true, but if advisors don't know what to do and
say, or how to finesse information, when they do get in touch
with clients, the results will be fair at best. Eric won people
over with his expertise, personality, patience, perseverance,
politeness, and professionalism. But none of this would have
been enough if Eric hadn't also had a plan for managing
his clients.

This chapter provides an eight-point plan for managing
client relationships. It includes detailed instructions on what
to do and how to communicate more effectively to keep the
relationship strong, how to size up each client account (is
it a win-win, win-lose, lose-win, or lose-lose?), and how to
approach each. It teaches you how to find opportunities in
conversations with current clients for introductions to people
who are ready to make a change.

VOLATILITY IS THE NEW NORMAL

The business officially changed in the summer of 2008. When
the subprime mortgage debacle nearly put the U.S. economy
into a depression, and clients lost a significant amount of

their net worth, many people blamed their advisors. Why, these clients wanted to know, hadn't their advisors foreseen the crisis and done something about their portfolios in time to save them?

Years later, the Dow is creeping up incrementally, not dramatically. Volatility is the new normal. The market can swing up or down 300 points in a day, and no one can really explain why. This is frightening to many investors—so many that advisors frequently come to me panicking about how to deal with nervous, demanding clients. I always say:

"Is this client a trader or an investor?"

Once you can answer that question about a client, you can figure out how to deal with him—or with any client who is worried by everyday changes in the market that are beyond any advisor's control.

First, answer these questions about yourself. Are you:

- Struggling with the ebbs and flows of the market?
- Trying to move clients and prospects who are sitting on the sidelines?
- Working with prospects who have their money in cash?
- Struggling with the perception that everyone in the business is a crook?
- Feeling that the industry itself has been tarnished?
- Hearing that people have lost their faith and trust in the business?
- Feeling that people are losing faith in you as an advisor?
- Thinking about getting out of the business?

How many of these questions did you say yes to? Whether you said yes to one or to all of them, welcome to the club. You are not alone. You do have some options. These are your choices. You can:

- Get out of the business.
- Continue to take the heat.
- Hunker down with your current clients, secure the assets you have under management, and stay away from developing new relationships.

Or:

- Embrace the new normal and seize the opportunity, as Eric did.

The savviest and most successful advisors, like Eric, see this window as a great opportunity and have had their best years ever since 2008.

I was a keynote speaker at the UBS national sales meeting recently, and I listened to Bob McCann, CEO of UBS Wealth Management Americas, speak to his troops. What he said really resonated with me because it reinforced what I thought and what Eric was doing. He said,

"As we face the most challenging economic times in our lives, now more than ever is actually the best opportunity for advisors to be in the advice business."

I could not agree more. Clients and prospective clients are confused, worn out, and exhausted by all of the economic news they hear. What they are looking for now is a partner, someone they can count on to help them make some of the biggest decisions in their lives. That partner can be *you*!

EIGHT-POINT COMMUNICATION PLAN TO GIVE CLIENTS WHAT THEY WANT MOST IN A RELATIONSHIP NOW

When asked what was most important to them in their relationships with their advisors—performance, fees, communication, or proper asset allocation—an overwhelming majority of clients surveyed chose communication.

You probably already know, and have been told many times, too, how important it is to communicate with your clients frequently. But what do you say when you do communicate with them, and how often should you be doing it? The elements of a successful plan are given here—you should tweak it according to your knowledge of your clients' tolerance.

1. Display Confidence

People use you partly because you make them feel better about their investments, and that feeling comes from their belief that you understand the market. It also comes from how you communicate your feelings about the present and the future. So when you believe that someone's portfolio is fine as it is, speak with confidence and conviction. Your clients need to know that *you* really believe what you are telling them. If you think they need this reminder, you can tell them (as Eric did) that their portfolio is in good shape—but that if you had acted on their suggestions when they were getting nervous, it would not be.

If you think changes need to be made—for example, that the portfolio needs to be rebalanced—communicate that confidently, too, providing logical explanations with visuals and details. If you don't know, or if you think you know, but you aren't quite sure, ask a colleague for a second opinion, then communicate with the client.

Eric spoke to his clients in a calm, matter-of-fact way. He delivered the information using graphs and details with self-assurance and belief in the strategy that was very reassuring to his clients.

2. Have a Positive Attitude

People can sense when you are excited about something and when you are troubled, afraid, or desperate. People need an advisor who is positive—everyone gravitates to positive people. Positive thinking is infectious; people want to work with a winner and be a part of winning. Be that positive person.

If things continue to be volatile and you express fear or concern, your clients will panic. Meet with or speak to clients only when you are feeling genuinely positive and upbeat. If you provide a positive point of view with a calm, confident demeanor, and explain it logically, as Eric did, your clients will feel a lot better about their situation. This upbeat attitude may not be reflected in their current financial statements, but at least they will feel they are in good hands, with a competent person who is the right advisor for them.

3. Demonstrate Leadership

I believe that this, more than anything else, is what clients are looking for from you. They want to see you take the initiative and demonstrate with actions, not words, why they should believe in you. If you lead properly, they will follow. This is exactly what Eric is doing, and it is paying off—he is receiving excellent referrals because of the actions he has taken.

His clients have lost confidence in the market and in our country's political leadership, too. They watch CNN, CNBC, and local news and read *USA Today*, focusing on the headlines. Their heads are spinning, and doubt creeps in. Many successful advisors tell their clients that if they watch long enough, they will hear news or analysis that validates their fears—there is always something to worry about.

However, there is always something to be hopeful about, too, and your clients need to hear and sense from you that things will be okay, that the financial sun will rise again.

You are the expert here, and you need a good bedside manner as much as a doctor who is delivering bad news does. If a doctor who was timid and had no personality said that your daughter had a serious ailment, and said it coldly, relaying only the facts, how would you feel? What if a more confident doctor told you the same news, but wrapped it in words that reassured you—that he'd treated children with this condition often before, and that, based on his experience, he was confident that your daughter would be fine after treatment? Would you feel differently?

The situation is the same in both cases, but in the second scenario, you as a parent would probably feel more optimistic and less worried.

Your clients are worrying, too—and that's why your leadership ability is mission-critical for your relationship with them.

4. Be Proactive

Do not wait for clients to call you. Take a look at your current list of clients and prepare a set schedule for calling to hold their hands. Now more than ever, you should be communicating more, so that clients not only know what is going on, but know that you care. I recommend calling your A list clients once a week or every other week. Call your B list clients at least once a month, and call your C list clients at least once every three months.

Don't wait for bad news or changes. If your clients' portfolios are in good shape compared to the industry average, let them know that. Unless you do, they will believe that what's happening in the financial news is happening to their portfolios. When you keep them abreast of where they are proactively, you're sending a strong message: that you are on top of things and are looking out for their best interests, even when they don't call and ask you to do anything.

5. Cite History

Clients can lose perspective. If they do, tell them about other recessions and about how and when the market came back. There are some great graphs online that show these historical trends clearly; these can be a big help to advisors who are trying to put things in perspective and provide a frame of reference for clients. Find some you like and share them with your clients.

6. Educate

You need to provide more information than ever before to get people comfortable with either staying in the market or investing more with you. Start by looking at your clients' portfolios and comparing them to the S&P and the industry average. Most successful advisors have beaten the S&P over the past few years—when the average portfolio was down 25 to 30 percent, their clients' portfolios were either slightly up, flat, or down only 10 percent.

When their clients realized that they were better off than most, their mood changed, and communications between clients and advisors became constructive again. If your clients, too, are beating the S&P and the industry average, tell them so. This will reinforce your clients' good feelings about you and your abilities, and they will realize that they are a lot better off working with you than they would be on their own or with someone else.

If your results are *not* better than the industry averages, do not bring up these statistics.

Another important part of education is to tell clients what you think is going on in the markets based on facts, or what you have learned by following and listening to experts—from PIMCO CEO Mohamed El-Erian to the *Wall Street Journal* and other sources that you respect. After 2008, people are still skeptical and worried about another meltdown. If your clients are worried about that, you need to explain, with examples, why that won't happen.

You may want to consider including these points:

- The banks are significantly stronger, and there are now mechanisms in place to identity issues and react much more quickly.
- In 2008, we did not know the extent of the banking problems until it was too late.
- Lack of political leadership is an issue.
- The politicians' polarized approach isn't solving our economic problems—we need reform if the markets are to grow. Until the politicians come up with an acceptable bipartisan plan, we will continue to have big swings in the market.
- Corporations are flush with cash, but they are sitting on the sidelines rather than investing in the United States. They are particularly reluctant to add payroll.
- The uncertainties in Europe continue. Until the Europeans stabilize their own debt crisis with a cogent and acceptable plan, the day-to-day markets here as well as there will have huge swings.

National discount clothing retailer Sy Syms had a great slogan: "An educated consumer is our best customer." That applies to the wealth management arena, too. Constantly educate your clients on what is happening, and share your perspective on what's going to happen in the future. When you share this information, your clients will become more comfortable letting you make decisions on their portfolios.

7. Provide New Ideas

Right now, everyone is willing to listen to a new, fresh idea. Not much new wealth is being created, and therefore you and your colleagues are all going after the same opportunities—people who already have advisors. When you get a new client, chances are that you are taking business away from someone else. Keep thinking of fresh and new ideas and sharing them with your clients and prospective clients. They may not say yes to all of them, but the fact that you have these ideas shows that you are working for and thinking of your clients, staying on top of things.

Sharing your ideas is another way to have a touch point with clients and prospective clients. Your ideas may come from colleagues, wholesalers, investment meetings, internal sources, or media. Whatever their source, you need to constantly be looking at your clients' portfolios and thinking about new ideas for improving them.

8. Let Them Know That They Are Not Alone

When clients watch the news or when they get a monthly statement and see that their portfolio is down, many of them respond emotionally. They personalize the statement and feel that nobody knows their sorrow or cares about it. So you need to let them know that you are in this with them, in it for the long haul. That may sound simplistic and insincere, but it is not. Your clients want and need to hear that you are there for them—that you are in this together and will get through this together.

Just saying these things to your clients will give them some comfort and a better feeling. Believe me, if you have not said anything like that to your clients yet, you need to do it immediately. If you don't, they won't just listen to ideas from other advisors—they will probably leave you for other advisors.

PRUNE YOUR BUSINESS

Periodically, you need to evaluate your current client relationships and make some difficult decisions. Are you spending too much time with clients who are always complaining, never happy, depressing you, or practically driving you crazy? If so, you may need to get rid of those clients.

Firing a client is certainly not the best feeling in the world as you're doing it, but sometimes you just have to do it—for the sake of your other clients, or for your own sanity. When Eric and I went over his client list, he learned to look at his clients in a new way, and then determine who should remain a client and who should not.

Here is what Eric did. You can use these criteria to look at your client relationships and see who the keepers are and who you should consider eliminating.

Win-Win

These are the clients that you like and that like you. You know they will be with you through good times and bad times because they believe in you. These clients truly value your advice, their relationship with you, and what you do for them. They thank you for what you do and tell you how much they appreciate it. They never question your fees; they never complain when things go awry. What percentage of your book falls into this category? Eric had 60 percent of his clients in this category. These clients are keepers.

Win-Lose

These clients are like your win-win clients in the sense that you have a nice relationship with them and they appreciate you. However, with these clients, that relationship comes at your expense. Maybe they get you to reduce your fee. Maybe they're always looking for perks—golf balls or favors— although they ask with a smile or even a joke.

For the most part, these clients are good people, and you get along well with them, but you know that you have to give in to their demands if you are to make them happy. Eric said that 25 percent of his clients were in this category. What percentage of your book is in this category? I feel that these clients are keepers, too. If you find that they are becoming too demanding and that you are spending an inordinate amount of time with them, they may slip into the next category. Only you can decide what "an inordinate amount of time" is.

Lose-Win

These are the clients who always feel that they are getting shortchanged. They are not happy with the way things are going, they complain a lot, and they feel that you are benefiting at their expense. They do not take your advice, and yet when things go wrong, they blame you. They drain your time and sap you of energy whenever you talk with them—making them happy is a Herculean effort. Do you have any clients that fit into this category? Eric felt that 10 percent of his book was in this category. We decided that he had to work on these relationships and get these clients to at least win-lose. If he couldn't, I advised him to terminate his relationships with them.

He agreed, except for one lose-win client: the daughter of one of his win-win clients. You should get rid of most of these clients, too—if you make exceptions, don't make too many.

When you discuss the possibility of terminating a client relationship, it is important that you stay unemotional and explain your reasoning clearly, politely, and professionally. Say something along the lines of:

> "_____, we need to talk. Do you have a few minutes? I sense that you have been unhappy with the way things have been going with your portfolio and our relationship for some time, and I want to talk about it, because I am not happy either. In order for us to continue to work together, I think we need to do certain things differently, such as _____ [try to keep this list neutral and express it in terms of specific behaviors].

> "Now, if for some reason you do not agree with me, I am prepared to introduce you to another advisor—perhaps you will be happier with him. What are your thoughts?"

One of two things will happen: either the client will agree with you and you will end the professional relationship, or the client will want to keep you as his advisor. In that case, the client will be receptive to what you propose that needs to take place going forward. This is what I refer to as the threat of the takeaway. Sometimes people need to realize that they cannot continue going on the way they have been, and the thought of losing you just may be enough to get them to change their behavior and get the relationship where you want it to be: to win-win or at least win-lose. Always make sure you part on good terms. Be as gracious, professional, and polite to them as you were when they were prospects. Treat them right because you never know what the future will bring. They may come back and become clients again, but on your terms, or they may be good referral sources. Either way, it does not matter. Follow the golden rule; treat people the way you want to be treated.

Lose-Lose

These are the clients who are usually unhappy, complain a lot, threaten to leave, and call whenever the market has a big swing. These clients can be rude, even nasty, to you and your team. They think they are always losing in the relationship.

If you have clients like this, you know you can never make them happy. You dread taking their calls or spending time with them. In addition, you feel that you have done everything you can to change things and that the relationship is not and will never be where you want it to be. In short, the client is not happy, and neither are you. Eric said that 5 percent of his clients fell into this category. What percentage of your business comes from people like this? Whatever it is, *end these relationships.* Either by phone or in person, let these clients know that you feel you have done everything you can for them, and it is clear that they are not happy. Suggest that they look for another advisor [use the previous script as a guideline, but don't offer to try to work on the relationship; you've already done that!]. Once you end these relationships, you will feel better, have more time to spend with your other clients, and have the energy to follow what you have learned so far in this book. You will then meet more people who can become win-win clients.

OPPORTUNITY IS KNOCKING—
LISTEN AND RESPOND TO THE SELLING CUE

Okay, so you have followed the eight-point plan and pruned your business; now what? You are about to have some interesting conversations with clients. You are going to get reactions from your clients one way or the other, and if you get positive reactions, you need to have a response ready.

Suppose, when you discuss the market and their portfolios with your clients, you hear responses such as these:

- "I am in your corner."
- "I appreciate all that you do for me."
- "Thank you."
- "Enough about me; how you are doing?"
- "I am not going anywhere."

- "We'll get through this together."
- "I am in it for the long haul, and you are doing a great job for me."
- "The downturn in the market is not your fault."

Opportunity is knocking at your door. This is the perfect time to ask for a referral. You need to seize the opportunity and respond in a way that sets the stage for you to be introduced to a prospect who meets your profile and is ready to become a client.

Here are two scripts that Eric has used in response to those statements. They have produced countless referrals and more than $1 billion in net new assets for Eric and others.

Script 1

"Thank you. I really appreciate your confidence, trust, and kind words.

"In good times, I certainly earn my keep, but times like we are in now are where I really earn my money. That being said, if there are people you know who are venting to you about their current situation, I would welcome an introduction just so that they are aware of me as a resource."

Or:

"Thank you. I really appreciate your confidence, trust, and kind words.

"Are there people you know who are venting to you about their current situation? If so, would you be comfortable making

an introduction on my behalf just so that they are aware of me as a resource?"

Either way, continue with:

"Great; how would you suggest we do this—a dinner or a phone call? You tell me what you are comfortable with."

Script 2

"Thank you. I really appreciate your confidence, trust, and kind words. In these tough times, I feel that what we do has more value to people like yourself who are _____ [fill in the blank here by stating the type of clients that fit your profile]. And I want to meet them through people I know through warm introductions made on my behalf. My question to you is this: would you be comfortable either introducing me to or giving me the contact information for someone you know who meets my profile so that now, more than ever, this person knows and is aware of me as a resource?"

I promise that if you use that script when opportunity is knocking, you will start getting introductions to more people. I encourage you to go back to Chapter 5 and look at the referral scripts there to prepare yourself for these conversations and meetings.

The Four Categories of Referrals

The people you meet through this kind of referral ask will fall into four categories. By understanding which one best describes the referral's current situation, you will know what your chances are and how much time you should devote to each of them.

Growth. This person has recently had a liquidity event: divorce, inheritance, or sold a company—she has what some people refer to as "money in motion." This person will probably be deciding where to invest her money within the next three months. This is the kind of person and opportunity to which you should be devoting a lot of your time. Communicate with people like this every week, because they will be making a decision soon. The more time you spend with this prospect, the greater the chances of getting her business. This kind of prospect is worthy of your immediate time and attention.

Trouble. This person is either personally unhappy with his current advisor or unhappy because his portfolio is in bad shape as a result of his advisor's bad advice— perhaps even investment management malpractice. Your client may have told you that this person made some bad decisions about his advisor, CPA, or estate attorney. The person may be going through a divorce or some another unfortunate event. For some reason, though, this person welcomes and needs your wisdom, guidance, expertise, help, and attention. I'd invest a great deal of time and attention in this person; someone in this situation is probably going to make a change. If you manage this opportunity properly and help the person deal with whatever crisis he is experiencing, you will be the beneficiary and become the new advisor.

Even keel. When you are connected with this person, you learn that she is happy with the way things are, even though you see things differently. She tells you up front that she doesn't need or want to make sudden changes. In fact, she is not highly motivated to make any changes. I do not care how good a salesperson you are—this person is not going to become a client of yours anytime soon. I would not put this person on my prospect list, although I would keep her on my radar and touch base every six months. There really is not much more you can do when a person has no compelling reason or motivation to make a change, so do not invest any more time than this.

Overconfident. When you meet this person, he starts bragging about how great things are, how his advisors are the smartest and best in the business and his returns are Madoff-like. Chances are that this person is not telling you the whole story. However, don't make the mistake of challenging him—that is not the way to start a relationship. Instead, come across as a good listener who is smart (reread Chapter 8 if you need to hone your listening skills). I recommend calling this person every quarter and continuing to listen, because people who are that overconfident often get into *trouble* quickly and easily. When this happens, you want to be on the other end of the phone—and clearly there to help. Because you have been such a good listener already and you know his situation, the overconfident person will feel comfortable telling you his new troubles.

In closing, you need to embrace the new era of volatility being normal. Do not run from it. Advisors who embrace the new volatility have excellent retention rates and happy clients. Advisors who run and hide are vulnerable. The question is, which kind of advisor are you going to be?

8

Improving Your Efficiency and Effectiveness

"What gets measured gets done."

Marcia, whose niche was working with multigenerational high-net-worth families, had sky-high confidence in herself. She was skeptical about this plan at first, but once she put together the road map and incorporated the sales pipeline and time management tools to keep her organized, she made up her mind to exceed expectations. Her strategy was to immediately start asking people in her network for warm introductions to high-net-worth people. Her practice almost immediately took off. She explained it by saying,

"Once I had the tools I needed to keep me on plan, everything else fell into place."

When it comes to managing their day-to-day routines and being more productive, advisors' most common concerns are organizing their sales activity, instilling more discipline and accountability into their practice so that they stay on task, and having enough time to do their jobs.

This chapter provides referral and networking process management tools to help you stay on task and achieve great results. Powerful accountability systems combined with determination promote results like Marcia's. As Paul O'Neill, former Treasury secretary and chairman of Alcoa and the RAND Corporation, once said, "Great process gives you great results."

ROLLING OUT YOUR WINNING MORE BUSINESS PLAN

If you have read the preceding chapters and want to get started, great. Marcia was eager, too. She began by going back to the beginning and completing all the previous steps, which took a few weeks. We allowed for this in the timeline we set up (see Table 8-1), and we included benchmarks to make sure she completed the tasks in a reasonable period of time.

Here is what Marcia did:

Week 1. Marcia created her objective, strategy, and accountability metrics as described in Chapter 1. Give yourself a week to put yours together—but don't procrastinate or let doing this take more than a week. It is

Table 8-1 Timeline for Marcia's Plan

	Build Road Map	Create A, B, C, and D Lists	Refine and Customize Scripts	Speak to Clients and Contacts	Speak to Referrals	Meet with Referrals
Week 1	X	X				
Week 2		X	X			
Week 3				X	X	
Week 4				X	X	X
Week 5				X	X	X

important that you get started right away, while your goal is still fresh in your mind. I realize that you are busy, but you can always rationalize delay. Remember: what separates the top performers from the rest is behavior change. In order to get the results you want from this process, you need to start right here, right now. Do not delay.

Week 2. Marcia's list of contacts and clients totaled 1,000. If your list is this long, it will probably take you about two weeks to categorize everyone as belonging on your A, B, C, or D list. Even if your list is shorter, I recommend giving yourself two weeks to put it together. That way, you can make sure that it's scrubbed and tight. This list is like a bank account—you will get out of it what you put into it. Give it some thought and time. During those same two weeks, you can do what Marcia did: start looking at the scripts in this book and working on creating your own. During this second week, Marcia also role-played with her team, so that by the time she went live in the third week, she was ready. I recommend that you do that too.

Years ago, as a VP of sales, I was invited to review Houghton Mifflin's sales training material, and the instructor used an analogy that has stuck with me when it comes to scripting and role playing. At the time, the Boston Celtics were one of the best teams in the NBA, and the instructor cited their best player to illustrate a point when he said, "Larry Bird does not go from his car to start the game. He warms up and practices the shots he will take during the game, so when the time comes he is warmed up and ready."

The same thing applies to you. Before you have that first conversation with a client or contact, prepare for it by practicing. Practice makes perfect.

Week 3. By this time, you should have your road map set, know whom you will ask for a warm introduction, and be ready to have those conversations. Many times advisors tell me that they have trouble finding the time to make those calls. Later in this chapter, you will be shown how to set up time blocks so that this will not be an issue going forward. Marcia's goal was to ask for introductions three times a week, and she expected to receive two names per week. She asked properly, and she ended up receiving four referrals the first week. She exceeded her own expectations, and the immediate results motivated her to devote more time to the process, which led to even more referrals and first meetings and greater pipeline activity, too. You may achieve even better results.

Weeks 4 and 5. By this time, your referral networking process should be humming along. During your revenue-producing hours, you should be spending time speaking to contacts and clients to receive warm introductions, calling referrals to set up your first meetings, and actually having those meetings. I know it sounds simple, and almost too good to be true, but if you follow the plan, it really will be that easy for you. Marcia found herself having an average of four referral meetings per month. Everyone's practice is different, but if you follow this plan, you will receive more qualified referrals than you do now.

USING PIPELINE MANAGEMENT
TO ORGANIZE YOUR SALES FUNNEL

As you follow the plan, you will have many prospects, clients, and opportunities to pursue. Few advisors track and manage their activities and opportunities effectively. Marcia certainly didn't until I recommended that she use simple homemade spreadsheet shown in Tables 8-2 to 8-4. You may prefer an Excel spreadsheet or a sales force automation tool or a CRM software package—it doesn't matter what you use, as long as you have an organized approach to manage your activity and use it regularly. Marcia created and used three tabs. A discussion of the fields in each tab follows.

First Tab: People I Want to Meet, but Have
Not Scheduled or Qualified Yet

Prospective client and referred by. These are people you want to have as clients. Either you know them by name and want to meet them, or a client or contact has offered to introduce you to them, but has not yet done so. Either way, start the process by capturing their names and how you got them.

> *Week of.* This pipeline should be updated and saved weekly. That keeps the process moving forward consistently, so that tracking prospects becomes second nature. As Vince Lombardi said about winning, "It needs to be an all the time thing—it can't be a sometimes thing."

Net asset $. If you know what the person's assets are, enter it in this field. If you do not know, enter TBD (to be determined).

Origin or status. Enter either where things started or where they are at the moment. For example, maybe you want to meet a client's friend, and your next step is to ask your client to set up a meeting. Marcia invited her client Greg Miller to a wine-tasting event and asked him to bring someone he knew who was also in a family business. Greg brought Ned Francis. Marcia spent a little time with Ned at the event and felt that they really hit it off, but she did not press him for a follow-up meeting. She decided that she would ask Greg later for Ned's contact information and his advice on the best way to proceed. Be explicit as you fill in your tabs, and make everything action-oriented. Your goal is to move the people from the first tab into the second tab, and what you put in this field should drive some form of activity to move things forward (or not because of a delay in scheduling, or for some other reason).

Second Tab: In Development—Qualifying, Scheduling, or Scheduled First Meeting with Prospective Client

Your goal is to move people from your On Radar tab into the next tab, In Development (Table 8-3). When you do that, you know that you are communicating with referrals, getting

Table 8-2 First Tab: On Radar—People I Want to Meet, but Have Not Scheduled or Qualified Yet

Week of _____

Prospective Client	Referred By	Net Asset $	Origin—Status
Jay Jarvis	Michael Smith	TBD	Need to ask Michael to set up golf game.
Cameron Smith	Michael Smith	$20M	Michael's brother; they work together. Expecting my call. Will call by 1-23.
Evan Teller	Sarah Fox	TBD	Called Sarah; waiting for call back.
	Greg Miller	TBD	Going to ask Greg for referral at client review on 1-12.
Ned Francis	Greg Miller	TBD	Met at wine tasting last week. Need Greg to get me his contact information.

them to meet with you, and driving your process forward. How many people you move indicates how well you are doing.

Prospective client. This is where you put people from the first tab who either have agreed to meet with you or with whom your client or contact is making arrangements for a first meeting or conversation.

Type. What type of relationship is the prospect looking for? This is based on either information from your client or contact, or a conversation you have had with the prospect. Marcia used IM for investment management, FP for financial plan, and FO for family office. You, of course, can come up with whatever initials you want to use that will help you look at the situation and get a quick snapshot of what the opportunity is about.

Status—action to be taken. After each conversation or meeting, you should be planning some form of future activity to drive the opportunity and determine whether it is viable or not. This field should indicate what has taken place and what the next steps are. For example, Marcia was introduced to Josie Page through a client, Anna Rogers. At lunch, Josie said that her money was being managed by a cousin whom she neither liked nor trusted, but because he was family, ending the relationship could take time. Marcia, realizing that this was a sensitive situation, decided to take the patient route: she suggesting meeting in a few months. As you can see from her notes, she captured this information so that when she looked at her pipeline, she could easily remember what had happened, see what she had to do next, and know when to do it. If you are working this plan diligently, you will have a lot of activity. This field will remind you what you need to do next and drive you to keep the process moving forward.

This field will also help you prioritize your time. Your goal with these In Development people is to look at this list every week and ask yourself what you can or will do to move these people from a first contact into a follow-up conversation or meeting and get them into the third tab, In Queue.

Third Tab: In Queue—Qualified Opportunities, Moving Forward and/or Making a Decision

The additional fields for this tab are percentage—the likeliness of the opportunity closing (percentage of close) and the discounted value. In order to gauge these fields properly you need to understand the Salmon Scale of Sensibility.

The Salmon Scale of Sensibility

Here you enter your estimate of the chances for success—how likely you think it is that the prospect will become a client. This helps keep you grounded concerning where things really stand. The suggested percentages for the various scenarios given here were taken from countless years of experience:

Table 8-3 Second Tab: In Development—Qualifying, Scheduling, or Scheduled First Meeting

Week of _____

Prospective Client	Referred By	Potential $ Amount	Type	Status—Action to Be Taken
Dave Gregg	Nellie Tucker	$2M	IM	Nellie scheduling dinner for the 3 of us for May.
Brian Shorter	Nellie Tucker	$5M	IM	Met Brian, good 1st meeting, sending financials.
Josie Page	Anna Rogers	$10M	IM	$ with cousin and is not happy. Suggested meeting in two months to keep communication going.
Jay Jarvis	Michael Smith	$3M	FP	Hit if off golfing. 1st meeting scheduled for May 15.
Cameron Smith	Michael Smith	$20M	FO	Wants me to meet wife; waiting to hear back for date.

IM = investment management
FP = financial plan
FO = family office

- *10 percent.* You had what you think was a good first meeting, but you are not sure, and you feel that you need another reading on this person to make a better assessment as to whether she is a real potential client or not.
- *25 percent.* You had a good first meeting, and the person agreed to a second meeting on the spot. You felt that you really hit it off, you genuinely like the person, and you can see yourself working well with him.
- *50 percent.* The first and/or second meetings went better than planned. Then the prospect responded to whatever follow-up you agreed on in a timely manner, sent you the financials as promised, and perhaps called you and wants you to meet with his spouse, his CPA, or his attorney.
- *75 percent.* You have had several meetings, and the prospect is sending you buying signals as described in Chapter 6. Your instincts tell you that she is going to become a client—now it's just a matter of time.
- *90 percent.* The prospect has signed the paperwork or told you that he wants to work with you and become a client.

Percent of closure. This is a barometer of how likely it is that this person will close and become a client. This is a more accurate reading on where you are with the prospect. The percentages you entered on the Salmon Scale of Sensibility are merely estimates. You may alter the percentages there based on other factors, including your gut feeling. Here, though, regardless of how you arrive at the percentage, the important thing is that you are honest and realistic about your chances of getting the prospect to become a client and not inflate what the opportunity truly is, because at the end of the day, it is your book of business, and it is not a tool to show anyone else how great things are or are not.

Discounted dollar value. This is the potential dollar amount times the percentage of closure. Many advisors look only at the potential dollar amounts, which can be very misleading. Advisors who look only at potential dollars, ignoring the fact that they may not close many of their prospects, have an unfortunate tendency to slip into neutral, falsely assuming that they have plenty in the pipeline and will do just fine. That's the wrong way to think about things! The total in the discounted dollar field is a much more accurate reading of where you stand and what might possibly close. My experience is that, on average, advisors bring in 60 to 75 percent of their discounted dollar amounts.

Totals. The totals of the potential dollar amounts and the discounted dollar amounts.

This tab is where you track your qualified opportunities. Once a prospect has told you that he's interested in exploring the possibility of working with you, has asked you for a proposal, has provided you with his financials, or has done something else to indicate his interest in working with you, he becomes a qualified opportunity. His name can be removed from the second tab and placed into the first field here. Not everyone you meet makes it to this tab. It is okay for someone to remain in the first or second tab, or you can take her off all together if and when you decide that she is no longer a prospect.

The best advisors use this pipeline and are constantly moving people from "On Radar" to "In Development" and then to "In Queue." See Table 8.4. These advisors stay organized and exceed their annual goals. You will, too, if you make the use of this pipeline management tool part of your routine.

INCORPORATING TIME MANAGEMENT TO GET THE MOST OUT OF YOUR DAY

Time management is always one of the biggest challenges whenever advisors have responsibilities other than bringing in new assets (new clients). Finding and maintaining balance in your life, plus getting to all the mission-critical things you need to do to become and/or remain successful, is not as easy as it may seem.

Most advisors struggle with time management, and when they do, some aspect of their business suffers—business development, proper asset allocation, or client retention activities. Table 8-5 shows a time management plan that has been praised by many advisors for the difference it has made and the results it has produced. Many of the *Barron's* best that I coach use a plan very much like this one.

The time blocks in Table 8-5 are shaded to call your attention to various aspects of time planning to help you differentiate among tasks. Remember, when it comes to being responsible for "putting points on the board," you are the only one who can drive your business—you are the only one

Table 8-4 Third Tab: In Queue—Qualified Opportunities, Moving Forward and/or Making a Decision

Prospective Client	Referred By	Type	Potential $ Amount	% Close	Discount $ Value	Status—Action to Be Taken
Marcia Price	Dan Black	IM	$5M	50%	$2.5M	Had two good meetings. Meeting again on 4-29.
Holly Keefe	Dan Black	IM	$2M	75%	$1.5M	Waiting for paperwork.
Neil Rodman	Alex Norton	IM	$1M	50%	$500K	On vacation. Being introduced to his CPA in 2 weeks.
Jay Jarvis	Michael Smith	IM	$2M	10%	$200K	Scheduling follow-up meeting. Tough guy to read.
Cameron Smith	Michael Smith	IM	$10M	90%	$9M	Loves what I do for family biz; funds to be transferred 5-2.
Totals			$8M		$5M	

IM = investment management
FP = financial plan
FO = family office

Table 8-5   Time Management for Advisors

7:00– 8:30 a.m.	Your time
	Organize and prioritize your day: track your short-term and long-term goals; make important or time-sensitive phone calls and e-mails
8:30– 10:00 a.m.	Anyone's time
	Breakfast meetings, internal meetings, client meetings, brainstorm, meet with team, communicate with support personnel, and so on.
10 a.m.– 3:00 pm	Client management and selling time
	Business development, external meetings, relationship building, identifying the champions, lunches, meetings with clients, prospects, phone calls, in-person meetings
3:00– 4:30 p.m.	Anyone's time
	Follow-up, internal meetings, brainstorming, strategizing, administration, and so on
4:30– 6:30 p.m.	Your time
	Phone calls, e-mails, expenses, proposals, entertaining, tracking short-term and long-term goals, preparing for the next day, and so on

who can put your best energy into your revenue-producing hours to make the maximum use of them.

Using this tool will help you take control of your day, improve your efficiency and effectiveness, and prevent unimportant matters from taking over your business.

7:00–8:30 a.m.: Your time. When Marcia arrives in the morning, she uses this time to get organized for the day and respond to time-sensitive things that require her immediate attention. She prioritizes, deciding what she wants or needs to do. During the day, you are probably responding to others—this is the time when you are in charge and you can set your priorities. Use this morning time to decide what gets done, and then, having decided whether you're going to plan for the day, read trade materials, make calls, return calls, read, or send and respond to e-mails, get started. Marcia started at 7 a.m. You may start later. The point here is that the first period of your scheduled day should be *"your time,"* and that is why you need to ensure that no one else interferes with what you need and choose to do. If you don't use it, other people will.

8:30–10:00 a.m.: Anyone's time. This morning time block should be considered a "jump ball." If anyone in the organization wants to see you, schedule the meeting for this time block. Marcia decided that she needed only 90 minutes to work with others on things like reviewing clients' portfolios with her CA, team meetings, proposals, pitch books, and meetings with her manager. Anyone's time is when you are open and available.

10:00 a.m.–3:00 p.m.: Client management and business development time. Marcia decided that she wanted to allocate five hours per day for this. Many other advisors allocate four hours either four or five days per *week* for this time, but Marcia believed that if she blocked off this time for clients, contacts, and referrals and used the time to manage relationships and prospects and develop new business opportunities, she'd see a huge payoff, which would equate to more assets under management, so that she would make more money. You too will see an increase in your pipeline activity simply because you consistently put in the time, and an increase in your referral opportunities simply because you asked for more warm introductions. Sales are a numbers game, whether you are targeting 6, 12, or 20 new clients. If you take the time to ask, and if you ask often enough, you will drive your own success (as long as you ask properly, following the instructions in this book).

3:00–4:30 p.m: Anyone's time. When you come back to the office after your client management and business development meetings, make yourself available again to others so that you can respond to the open items that have developed or things that your team has been working on where they need your involvement. Marcia decided that she needed only one hour, but most advisors allocate either 90 minutes or two hours. That way, anyone who needed to see you earlier but didn't get to do it now has another opportunity. This is a good time to either catch up on whatever has happened earlier in the day or schedule an internal meeting.

4:30–6:30 p.m.: Your time. The end of the day is a good time to respond to or initiate e-mails and calls that aren't time sensitive. Between 8:30 and 4:30, you were responding to others' needs. Now is another time to take care of your own needs and do things at your own pace.

Having a schedule and adhering to it are two different issues. Things that will disrupt your schedule and eat into your time are always going to come up. When a client can meet with you only during "your time," or when an unexpected deadline prevents you from using your client time to prospect, don't worry. And don't feel that you need to "double up" tomorrow for what you missed today.

Think of it like taking a prescription that calls for one pill per day. If you forgot to take it one day, would you take two pills the next? The same thing applies to your time management plan. Do not panic when your schedule blows up. Just attack it again the next day with focus and discipline—you'll get back on track.

The key to implementing and executing a time management plan is educating your support personnel, colleagues, and management that this is how you now are going to run your business. I recommend sitting everyone down, showing them the plan, and letting them know how important it is for you to stay on schedule. That's what Marcia did. You will know that they got the message when you overhear them saying things like, "We can't talk to her now; it is not 'anyone's time.'"

REPORTING TO A COACH AND EXCEEDING EXPECTATIONS

Most successful executives, and all successful athletes, have coaches. Phil Mickelson, recognized as one of the best golfers on the planet, employs Butch Harmon as his swing coach. Even without his coach, Phil would probably still be a great golfer—but would he be in the top 10 year after year without Butch? Phil doesn't think so. Butch shows him ways to improve his game and helps him practice them.

His work with this expert coach gives Phil confidence when he's competing. A coach can do the same thing for you. I work with Raj Sharma, a perennial *Barron's* top 20 advisor, and I once asked,

"Raj, you are so successful—one of the best in the business—why are we working together?"

"Because I feel I can still learn something from you," he said.

The point is that the best advisors, like the best athletes, are always refining their game. If coaching helps Phil Mickelson and Raj Sharma, it will pay major dividends for you, too.

Selecting the Right Coach for You

If you have a manager or director, your first reaction may be to select her as your coach. However, if you don't, you need to think who else may be available to you.

If your organization has a practice management team, ask if it has a business development resident expert. Perhaps your organization has a complex, district, or regional sales manager. One of these people may be qualified, too. Lastly, you may want to consider someone on your team or an external coach who specializes in working with advisors. Wherever you look, whomever you interview, be sure to consider these criteria:

- *Trust.* This is a gut feeling about someone.
- *Honesty.* This person will always tell you the truth.
- *Candor.* This person will be direct and will not "sugar-coat" things or hold back.
- *Reliability.* You know you can always count on this person.
- *Is demanding and willing to push you.* She will not accept "good enough."
- *Objectivity.* He is not beholden to you and knows the business.
- *Experience.* She has business development experience working with advisors.
- *Will not let you off the hook.* He will hold you accountable to your commitments.

What a Coach Will Do for You

First and foremost, what Marcia wanted from a coach was to help her instill accountability and discipline into her practice. This is what I refer to as the *quantitative* part of the coaching relationship. During our second coaching session with Marcia, I noticed a distinct difference in the velocity of her activity and her preparedness for our sessions. I asked her what she attributed this to. She said,

"I never had a coach before, and this has forced me to change the way I do things. I now have a road map with a clear objective and a strategy. I report to you how I am doing on asking clients and contacts and getting meetings with referrals—that's already produced results. Your holding me accountable for my commitments, and the fact that you told me that if I did not stick to it, I would lose you as a resource, was a great motivator." She continued, "Sticking to the time management program really helped, too. I now have more free time for other aspects of my job, and I am in a good rhythm. Lastly, I never had a pipeline tool that made it so easy to keep track of my activity. I see the results in black and white, and that motivates me to do even better. Now that I have been doing it every day for two months, this is my new routine."

Marcia truly took advantage of the practice management tools she was given, with great results. Having a good coach will force you to live up to your commitments, and before you know it, accountability will become part of your practice, too, if you are willing to embrace the concepts and have the discipline to change your behavior.

That starts with simple repetition. If you do the things described here every day, your third-month review results will be off the charts, as Marcia's were. A coach can help here, too: I told Marcia what she did well and then said, "This is great; now do more of it." She repeated her routine consistently, and she came to each of our meetings with updates from her pipeline. Her documented accountability results (results in black and white) showed that she had developed the discipline to be a top advisor.

Using the tools in this chapter and reporting to your coach about your progress will ensure that you achieve your goals and stay on track. Soon that discipline will be as much a part of your routine as shaving or brushing your teeth.

Marcia was also looking for support in the *qualitative* component of a coaching relationship: guidance, help, opinions, and validation that what she was thinking or doing made sense. Here are some of the things I worked on with Marcia that you may want to incorporate into your coaching relationship:

- *Strategize on opportunities at different stages to get a better outcome.* Your coach may give you a different perspective, give you a new approach to a situation, or simply confirm that your way is the best way. I worked with Marcia on pipeline management, and we brainstormed on everything from what to say to whom to bring to the follow-up meetings to questions to ask and ways to close.
- *Client retention and management.* If you tell your coach what's going on with each client relationship, he can help you solidify your relationships and perhaps point out ways to leverage those relationships for more wallet share and additional referrals.
- *Practice optimization.* Sometimes advisors are so close to situations that they need help being objective enough to make decisions. A coach can help with advice, suggestions, and solutions that you would never have thought of by yourself. Your coach can help you streamline your schedule so that you are constantly putting your time to its highest and best use. For Marcia, the time management part of our relationship became a game changer. It gave her more free time to spend with her children than she'd ever had.

- *Marketing and branding.* Your coach can take a fresh look at how you are represented in the marketplace. Advisors often have difficulty distinguishing themselves here because almost all advisors say the same things. Having a fresh, objective look at how you present yourself to others is beneficial, especially now, when people are willing to listen to new ideas. If you look and sound exactly like your peers, why would anyone even think about making a change?

- *Scripting and role-playing.* A good coach can help you customize the scripts in this book for maximum effect. Your coach can help you add your personality to the equation and help you find your voice so that the scripts sound natural and effective when you deliver them. Sometimes you may want to practice what you are going to say, and your coach is a good person to do this with.

- *Helping you make strategic decisions.* When you need to make a major decision, it helps to talk it through with someone who has your best interests at heart. Your coach can provide both a sound second opinion and objectivity. As Marcia said to me, "You tell me what I need to know, not what I want to hear." The more you allow your coach to become embedded in your business, the more your coach can do for you, including steering you toward better, more informed decisions.

- *Listen.* Sometimes your coach will listen just because you need to vent. This business is getting harder and more challenging all the time, and when you feel down but you need to be up for your clients and colleagues, having someone who's there for you can be a huge boost to your morale. I've taken many calls at 7 a.m. from *Barron's* top advisors when they just needed someone to listen; that helped them, and having a coach who listens can help you, too.

How Often Should You Meet with Your Coach?

A formal monthly session usually works best; as you implement the ideas in this book, you will be too busy to meet with a coach more often than that. If you can't meet in person, talk by phone. Alex Rodriguez, the baseball player for the New York Yankees, speaks to his personal coach daily at a set time before he goes to the ballpark.

When he is at home, they may meet in person, but when he is on the road, they do it by phone. The point is, he has a routine, and you need to establish one, too. Setting aside 60 to 90 minutes once a month, at a time when you won't be speaking with clients or prospecting for new ones, is perfect.

A good coach will make herself available to clients 24/7 with a guaranteed 24-hour turnaround via e-mail or phone. This is so that advisors do not have to wait to discuss time-sensitive issues. Ask your coach what her availability between sessions will be and come to a mutually acceptable time frame.

What Your Coach Will Expect of You

Your coach will have certain expectations. I expected Marcia to:

- Show monthly progress.
- Be prepared to discuss the quantitative aspects of her progress.
- Track her accountability metrics for asks, referral names, meetings scheduled, and new business closed.
- Review what was working and what was not so that we could dissect problems and come up with solutions.
- Review the sales pipeline.
- Work on strategies to move opportunities forward.
- Display honesty. Tell the truth, for better or worse.
- Live up to her commitments and promises.
- Not make excuses.
- Put forth the effort.
- Stay focused.

What I expected from Marcia is both straightforward and reasonable. Your coach will expect the same from you—and, in fact, needs it if he is to remain engaged. Most advisors begin plans like this with good intentions, just as most people begin diets with good intentions, and get the same results—they soon give up. Do not cheat yourself or your coach. Stick with it and you will succeed; cheat and you will fail. It's that simple.

9

Dealing with the What-Ifs

Brian, an advisor at a bank, wanted to discuss business with his neighbor, Mark. They both knew what the other did for a living but had never talked professionally. Brian was worried that if he broached the subject and it did not go well, he would become the guy people avoided because he talked business in social settings. I told him that opportunity is all about timing, equity in the relationship, and the approach. He told me he would see Mark in a few weeks at a barbeque.

We agreed if they were alone he would begin the conversation as he normally does by asking Mark about his family, what's new, and so on. If the conversation was going well, Brian should continue by saying something along the lines of, "Mark, you and

I have never talked business before. I'd love to talk shop with you over a breakfast or dinner one of these days. Would you be interested in doing that?"

Brian was very comfortable with that approach and executed it comfortably. Mark agreed to a breakfast, and over time they converted their personal relationship into a professional one and Brian's bank now manages Mark's company's 401(k) plan.

Situations like Brian's are going to come up that have not been covered so far in this book. Therefore, this chapter shows you how to handle the "what-if" questions that arise during the course of many advisors' day-to-day routines. What if you've left three voice mails already? What if you can't get past the admin? What if you think your e-mails are getting trashed unread? Dealing well with these and other situations that pop up in your business will make a big difference to both your pipeline and your peace of mind. This chapter gives time-tested responses—what to do, what to say, and how to do it or say it—that have yielded great results for other advisors in those situations.

WHAT IF I KNOW SOMEONE SOCIALLY AND I WANT HIM AS A CLIENT?

I call this mixing business with pleasure. Mixing business with pleasure is one of the greatest challenges for advisors. Trying to mix business with pleasure feels more unnatural, awkward, and uncomfortable than almost any other situation in this book. That's because the last thing you want is to be the person that everyone in your community, club, house of worship, or circle of friends runs away from—and your fear is that if you introduce business in these settings, people will run away from you.

How many times have you been in a social situation and thought something like,

> "I'd love to talk business with _____, but if I do, I might jeopardize our friendship."

> "_____ has so much money that I would love to talk shop, but I don't want people to think I'm pushy and avoid me."

> "I don't know how _____ would feel about my approaching her here."

Start by recognizing that there is a time and a place for everything. The opportunity to talk business with people you know socially is all about a few things.

- *The equity you have built up in your relationship with this person.* You have to earn the privilege of asking, and that takes time, effort, and commitment to the *relationship*, not the business opportunity. It doesn't work to coach a team or join a board strictly for the business opportunities it may provide. People will see through you, and your chances of ever having a personal relationship with anyone in the group, let alone developing that into a business discussion, will be slim.
- *How well you know the person.* One way to gauge this is to ask yourself about your history. If you've known each other for more than two years and you've never

asked before, you are fine. He will not be thinking, "So George has been lying in the weeds over the past few months, sitting on the board just so that he can hit me up." If you've known someone for years, that will not be his mindset, and if you speak with confidence and ask *properly* (making it comfortable for him to say no and dropping the subject if it's clear that that's what he wants to do), asking is a nonissue.

- *Timing.* If you are at a board meeting, a neighborhood party, the club, or some other social setting, ask only if:

  o The two of you are alone, engaged in a one-on-one conversation that no one else can hear.
  o The other person asks about your business.
  o You have already gone through the pleasantries.
  o You're alone and it's toward the end of lunch after a round of golf or you're walking out to the parking lot after a board meeting, flipping a burger on the grill, or saying good-bye at the end of a dinner party.

- *How you broach the subject.* Here are three different ways that usually work.

  Example 1: "_____, I was thinking about you the other day. You and I have never talked business before. I would love to get together for a breakfast or dinner to explore some ideas with you. Is this something you'd be interested in doing?"

  Example 2: "_____, I was thinking about you the other day. I know you are involved with _____, and I am at _____. I would love to talk shop with you over a breakfast or dinner. Would you be interested in doing that?"

Example 3: "_____, in all the time we have known each other, we have never spoken about business together. I know you are with _____, and I am at _____. We have done some work in the _____ area, and I would love to get together and share some ideas I have with you. Is that something you'd feel comfortable doing with me?"

If the person says yes, continue with:

"Great. What's a good day and time for you?"

If he says no or makes up an excuse, continue with:

"No problem. It was something I was thinking about that made sense to me, and I just wanted to ask."

WHAT IF I NEED TO LEAVE VOICE MAIL? MOST PEOPLE NEVER CALL ME BACK WHEN I DO THAT

Leaving voice mail that gets a response is an art. The voice mail needs to pique your recipient's interest, and the best way to do that is by being both brief and informative. What you say depends upon your relationship with the recipient. Here are some scripts that will almost guarantee a return phone call.

For a Client or Contact

Example 1: "Dana, this is Beth. I want to bounce an idea off of you. Could you please give me a call when you get back to the office?"

Example 2: "Dana, this is Beth. I'd like to speak with you when you have a minute. If you get this message before the day is out, could you please give me a call at the office at 5 p.m.?"

For a Referral

Example 1: "Hi, Frank. This is Beth Graham. Dana Cooper suggested I give you a call. I can be reached at 508-555-1213 later today and tomorrow. If that's not good for you, I will call you back on Friday morning at 10 a.m."

Example 2: "Hi, Frank. This is Beth Graham, Dana Cooper's friend. I am calling at Dana's request. Dana thought it would be a good idea for us to connect. I'll be around between 8 and 10 a.m. tomorrow. You can reach me at 508-555-1213. If I haven't heard from you by Thursday, I will call you back on Friday at 2 p.m."

Example 3: "Hi, Frank. This is Beth Graham. I had lunch with Dana Cooper earlier today, and she told me to call you directly. I wanted to schedule some time to speak when it is convenient for you. I will be around the rest of the day today and can be reached at 508-555-1213. If I have not heard from you in a few days, I will call you back on Friday at 2 p.m."

I have found that giving a specific deadline increases your chances that the person will call you back. There have been studies done that confirm this. Also, it allows you to start managing the process on your terms.

WHAT IF I HAVE TO SPEAK TO THE ADMINISTRATOR OR SECRETARY TO GET THROUGH TO THE REFERRAL?

Dealing with gatekeepers is not easy. The first rule is, develop a rapport with these individuals. Remember that keeping people away from their boss is part of their job description. However, these people are also human beings and generally will respond better if you treat them with respect and not disdain.

Always introduce yourself, ask for the person's name, and let him know that you really need his help. This will disarm many. If that doesn't work, mentioning your client, contact, or referral's name should neutralize him. Gatekeepers generally have no idea how well your client, contact, or referral knows the person you are trying to reach, or the relationship between them. The gatekeeper is fear-driven. Using this knowledge will get you what you need.

Here are two scripts that get the job done:

> *Example 1:* "_____, I need your help. _____ is a friend of mine and of _____'s [her boss]. He suggested that I connect with _____ [her boss] and speak with or get some time with him. Do you manage his calendar?"

If the gatekeeper says that she does not manage his cal-endar, say something along the lines of:

> "I could use your help. Do you think you can let Louis know I called, let him know that Mark wanted us to get 10 or 15 minutes on the phone, and ask when he can do that?
>
> "Great, thanks. When I should call you back to check?"

Example 2: "I am calling Louis at Mark _____'s request. Mark wanted the two of us to connect. Am I getting you at a good time?

"Do you manage his calendar? If so, can you please take a look over the next two weeks and let me know what's a good day and time for us to get 10 or 15 minutes on the phone?"

If the gatekeeper says that he does not manage his boss's calendar, say something along the lines of:

> "I could use your help. Do you think you can let Louis know I called, let him know that Mark wanted us to get 10 or 15 minutes on the phone, and ask Mark when he can do that?
>
> "Thanks much. When I should call you back to check?"

However, even with these new lines, you may get some pushback. Here are the two best ways to respond to them.

Responding When the Gatekeeper Says, "May I Ask What This Is in Reference To?"

"Louis suggested I call. If you could let Mark know that Louis wanted us to connect, that would be great. Please have him call me tomorrow at 10 a.m. at 968-875-0948. If not, I can call back on Friday morning."

You do not have to explain the reason for the call unless you feel a need to. It is not necessary. What is important is that you are polite, respectful, and professional.

Responding When the Gatekeeper Says, "If He's Interested, He'll Call You Back."

"I can appreciate that. And your name is? Sandy, Louis told me if Mark was not in that I should ask for you [provided this is true].

"I could really use your help here, as Louis mentioned that you manage his calendar. Do you think there would be a better time for me to call him back?"

The administrator's tone may change as a result of your approach. The administrator will not cause a problem once she understands that there is a relationship between you, a third party, and her boss. Chances are she has no idea of the origin or strength of the relationship, and once you present it that way, she won't want to take the risk of annoying her boss by offending you or his friend. That is just the way people in that position think.

WHAT IF OUR E-MAIL COMMUNICATIONS SUDDENLY END WITH NO EXPLANATION AND THE REFERRAL, CLIENT, OR CONTACT HAS NOT RESPONDED AFTER A FEW WEEKS?

Advisors complain or get frustrated when they've been working with someone and feel that they have a good rapport with her, and then all of a sudden everything stops. Some people call this "radio silence"; I call it "the Heisman" (after the Heisman Trophy, the award given each year to the most outstanding college football player, which has a statue of a player putting his hand out to STOP).

When you get the Heisman, you need to get things started again. Here are some e-mail subject lines that may well get a response:

- Following Up
- Touching Base
- Please Take a Look
- Do you have 5 minutes to talk this week?
- Information as Promised
- As Promised
- Thanks in Advance
- FYI
- Thought you'd want to know
- Need to speak to you
- Your thoughts

WHAT IF A CLIENT OR CONTACT
HAS OFFERED TO MAKE AN INTRODUCTION
BUT NOTHING HAS HAPPENED YET?

You can either call, e-mail saying you want to talk, or wait until the next time you meet. When you do talk, whether in person or over the phone, say something like this after the pleasantries:

Option 1
"_____, you mentioned that you wanted to introduce me to _____. Are you still comfortable with the concept of making that introduction on my behalf? And if you are, how should we do this—should we set up golf or a lunch? What's best for you? And when can we do that?"

Option 2
"_____, the last time we were together you mentioned you wanted to introduce me to _____."

Or:

"_____, the last time we were together you offered to introduce me to _____."

Either way, continue with:

"Are you still comfortable with doing that?"

"And if you are, how should we do this, golf, lunch, or you give me their contact information and I will call them?"

"What's best for you?"

If he says yes, respond with,

"When can we do that?"

Option 3
"_____, the last time we were together you seemed
to be receptive to making an introduction on my behalf?"

Either way, continue with:

"Are you still comfortable with doing that?"

"And if you are, what do you suggest for next steps?"

Or:

"And if you are, who do you have in mind and what do
you suggest for next steps?"

If he says yes, continue with,

"When can we do that?"

WHAT IF I HAVE A CONTACT WHO HAS A
NEIGHBOR OR FRIEND I WANT TO MEET?

First, try this only if you have a good relationship with the
person, so good that you are really friends. If you're friends,
you have enough equity in the relationship to ask. When

you do, sprinkle in an example of how another friend made a similar sort of introduction and it worked out well for all concerned. After the pleasantries, say something like:

> "Frank, do you know Don Best? How well do you know him? I would love to be introduced to him, the way Jack introduced me to Gary Davis. We ended up becoming friends, and he's been a client for a few years now. Would you be comfortable setting up a lunch for you, Don, and me?"

If your friend agrees, be sure to continue with questions like:

> "When should I get back to you on this?"

> "How well do you know Don?"

> "If you were me, how would you approach Don?"

WHAT IF ONE OF MY CLIENTS WORKS WITH OTHER PEOPLE I'D LIKE TO MEET?

This is a pretty straightforward ask. Here is the best approach. After the pleasantries, begin with:

> "Jeff, I would like to meet other Apple executives through a warm introduction."

> "Are there two or three colleagues of yours that you'd be comfortable making an introduction to on my behalf, just so that they are aware of me as a resource?"

If he says yes, don't forget to ask the follow-up questions:

"How do you suggest we do this? Do we set up a meal or golf, do you call, or do you just want to give me their contact information and I will call them?"

"What do you think is the best way to make this happen?"

"When should I get back to you on this?"

WHAT IF I WANT TO GET MORE "WALLET SHARE" FROM AN EXISTING CLIENT WHO HAS MONEY IN OTHER PLACES?

Either call or e-mail your client, let him know you want to speak to him, and schedule a specific day and time. After the pleasantries, be direct. Say something along the lines of:

Example 1: "You and I have been working together now for _____ years. My interest is in doing more for and with you. Realistically, what more do I need to do in order for the two of us to have that kind of conversation?"

Or:

Example 2: "You and I have been working together now for _____ years. My interest is in doing more for and with you. Realistically, what more do I need to do in order to have the opportunity to take on more of your investment portfolio?"

WHAT IF SOMEONE ASKS ME WHAT I DO?

Whenever someone asks you what you do, you have an opportunity that I call the "It Moment Pitch." You have up to 30 seconds (talk longer than that and you risk alienating the other person) to make a favorable and lasting impression. Be prepared with a pitch that will capture your target audience's interest and attention. Remember what Gordon Gekko said to Bud Fox in the movie *Wall Street*? "Life boils down to a few moments." When you get your chance, you must be ready!

Your pitch may vary depending on the venue or the circumstances. What you say in a social situation should be different from what you'd say in a business after-hours forum. But whatever the circumstances, answer these questions when planning your pitch:

1. What do you want people to know about you?
2. What distinguishes you and/or your firm?
3. What is your objective? In other words, what are you going to say to show this person that it is not about you but about her, and to get her talking beyond the pitch?

Here are two sample pitches that will help you prepare your own. In some situations, you will find yourself strictly talking business; in others, it's strictly pleasure; and then sometimes you are mixing both. It's a fine line, and you can't afford to overstep your boundaries in any type of scenario. The "pitches" you will read are guidelines, not scripts. Your pitch should incorporate your personality so that you come across as believable. I urge you to practice it until you get comfortable with it and it comes off naturally. Remember, you never get a second chance to make a first impression.

Example 1: For a Business and/or Social Setting

What do you want people to know about you? "I'm at Merrill Lynch."

What distinguishes you and/or your organization?
- "Been in the business for more than 16 years."
- "Manage wealth for retirees of publicly traded companies, retired business owners, and nonprofit organizations."

What is your objective? Ask, "What do you do?" to learn more about the person and make the conversation about her.

This advisor kept it short and simple and has a pitch that can be used in both business and social settings. Here is the script in its entirety:

"I'm at Merrill Lynch and have been in the business for more than 16 years managing wealth for retirees of publicly traded companies, retired business owners, and nonprofit organizations. What do you do?"

Example 2: For a Business Setting:

What do you want people to know about you? "I'm at Morgan Stanley Smith Barney."

What distinguishes you and/or your organization?
- "On a team with more than 50 years of experience."
- "Manage all financial matters for high-profile athletes, entertainers, divorcées, and widows, including but not limited to investment management, trust and estate work, and paying all of their bills."

What is your objective? "What you do sounds interesting. What are your biggest challenges these days?" Since the woman asking had already told the advisor what she did for a living, the advisor asked this question to get her to talk more about herself. Since this pitch was delivered in a business setting, this advisor provided a little more information than he would have used in a social setting.

Here is the script in its entirety:

"I am with Morgan Stanley Smith Barney on a team that has more than 50 years experience managing wealth for high-profile athletes, entertainers, divorcées, and widows. We get deeply involved in all of our clients' financial matters, from investment management and trust work to paying all of their monthly bills. Our high-touch service model gives our clients peace of mind so they can focus on what they do best. What you do sounds interesting. Tell me, what are your biggest challenges these days?"

This chapter covered some of the what-ifs that come up for advisors; I am sure you have others, too. Please do not hesitate to e-mail me at msalmon@salmonsays.com and I will help you with any what-ifs that have not been covered here.

10

Creating a Referral
Network for Life

SALMON SAYS

"Your network is pure gold. Nurturing it will increase
the value."

Congratulations! You've made it. The time and effort you've
put in following along up to this point has paid off, but you
still have a little more work to do. Have you ever taken a
golf lesson? Or been coached in dancing, snowboarding,
tennis, or skating? If you have, you may have noticed that
when the instructor is there, you do what he tells you to do,
and things go surprisingly well. However, when your coach
is not there, you revert to your old habits, because they feel
more comfortable—and things do not go as well as you
hoped they would. Then the instructor comes back, you
immediately start doing things his way, and even though it

feels a little uncomfortable, things go just as well as he told you they would.

That's true of what you've read in this book, too. If you have read the book and are now thinking, "This was great. I picked up a few new ideas and read some good stories. I really should start doing things as prescribed in this book," and then the book just sits on the shelf, guess what's going to happen? That's right, nothing will change. Everyone has intent. What separates the top performers from the rest is behavior change. If you do not change the way you do things, you will not have the success you want. That's the truth and the bottom line.

SO LET'S RECAP

You now:

- Have a plan, with a road map with clear objectives, supportive strategies, and a built-in accountability mechanism to keep you focused on networking activities.
- Have a clear mental picture of your client profile that makes it easy for your contacts and clients to introduce you to exactly the kind of people you want to meet.
- Know how to prioritize your clients and contacts; categorize them as A, B, C, or D; and leverage select social media outlets.
- Know whom to ask, when to ask, how to ask, and what to do after you ask clients and contacts for warm introductions to referrals.

- Have time-tested scripts that work for speaking to clients and contacts.
- Know how to do the necessary due diligence so that when you speak to a referral for the first time, you come across as credible, knowledgeable, empathetic, and resourceful.
- Know the step-by-step chronological order of the critical elements of a successful script for a first-time conversation and the next steps to convert these referrals into clients.
- Have a detailed plan to identify, cultivate, and optimize centers of influence relationships that will lead to more introductions and new client relationships.
- Have a plan to not only survive but thrive in these changing, volatile times and uncover additional referral opportunities.
- Have time management and sales pipeline tools to improve efficiency and effectiveness and instill more discipline and accountability into your practice.
- Are ready for the "what-ifs" that arise on a day-to-day basis.

NETWORKING IS NOT A SOMETIME THING, IT'S AN ALL-THE-TIME THING

If you do all these things, you will change not only the way you approach your business, but also the way you approach your life. The majority of people have heard the word *networking*; you now understand the concept, in depth. More important, you now know *how to* network. You can use your new skills to bring in more clients and net new assets for your organization and make more money for yourself. But that's just the beginning. Networking is a life skill that will change the way you function in the world and the way you build relationships from now on. With it, you are better equipped to handle life's challenges.

It is important that you keep your network fresh and up-to-date throughout your life. If you do, you will be able to accomplish anything you want, professionally or personally. Your life will become much easier. What do you think will happen if you don't maintain your network? Think about the differences between you and someone else whose network is larger and stronger. That person's ability to access people or information at a moment's notice makes him more efficient and effective than you are. Think of the time you've saved by knowing how to get results quickly because you've made valuable connections for life. You just have to make it a priority. Don't wait until it is too late. Get into the habit now.

GIVING AND RECEIVING—IT'S A TWO-WAY STREET

At the beginning of this process, you were the beneficiary of help from others. Now that you are an experienced networker, it is very important to remember what others did to help you attain success. You are now in a position to return the favor and help others when they are doing their own networking. If a particular event or occurrence makes you think of someone in your network, try to think of a way you can help that person, either personally or professionally. It does not have to be to "return the favor" or for a specific purpose. If you are always asking and never giving back, your network will become weak and inefficient. You will be a "taker," not a "giver." Do not let this happen to you.

A lifelong friend and contact of mine, Joe Grunfeld, is a senior person at Merrill Lynch Private Banking and Investment Group in New York. We had lost touch for many years, but we were reconnected through a mutual friend. Joe has helped me in many different ways with introductions both within and outside his organization. I have regularly asked him what I might do to help him, since I wanted to demonstrate my appreciation for all he has done for me. He said, "I just want to see you become successful, and I will help you in any way possible." Joe was not looking for anything in return. This is how your network should work if it is to be optimally effective.

Since Joe is on my C list, I communicate with him on a regular basis—at least once per quarter at a minimum. These discussions provide both of us with the opportunity to inform the other of what is happening in our respective personal and professional lives. Joe called me recently to ask if I could get him and his friends a table at Rao's. Rao's is one of the most exclusive restaurants in New York, and one of the hardest to get into. It does not take reservations. You have to know someone who has a table, and if she is not using it, you can get it for the evening. It took a few calls to select people in my network, but finally I thought of Sam, a B. Sam is in the wholesale meat business and does business with many restaurants. Sam made a few calls to his network. His friend John had a table, and we were able to get Joe into Rao's. This was one way I could express my appreciation for all Joe has done for me, and it is a perfect example of how a network should operate.

The P.S. to this story is that Joe went with a friend, Al, who has a very senior position at an organization I wanted to work with. Over dinner, Al asked Joe how they were able to get a table. Joe told him about his friend who is a SuperNetworker (me) and a little about my business. Al was impressed and said he wanted me to speak to me. His company is now one of my clients. These are the kinds of things that happen when you network for life.

Do not wait for someone to do you a favor before you do something for him. Be an initiator, not a reactor! If you step back from the hectic nature of everyday life and allow yourself a few minutes to reflect on the people in your network, you can easily think of something you can do for each person. Maybe it's just a phone call to stay in touch and learn how she, her family, and her business are doing. Everyone likes to feel wanted and important. You have the power within you to make someone feel special. Use it. There are many creative ways to show your appreciation for the people in your network. When you do, it sends a strong message that you really care about them. In return, people will be much more likely to help you when it is you who are asking for the favor.

Lastly, don't feel uncomfortable asking people for help or for a warm introduction, even if you haven't done anything for them. In the long run, things will even out. Asks are based on relationships, not the logic of "I should wait until I've done something for him." That is not the way the people you want on your side think. They know that it's not so much what you know as whom you know. These people will make introductions without weighing favors because that is the way they operate—if they can help someone, they do. If someone balks at your request, don't take it personally. The refusal simply means that the person you asked lacks the business maturity to think long-term. People who have lasting success in business know that building relationships is what it's all about. The sooner you embrace this concept and incorporate it into your day-to-day activity, the better off you will be, both personally and professionally.

Index

A

Accountability, in objective setting and strategy preparation, 13–15
Accountants, 25, 90–91
Accuracy, on LinkedIn, 35
Achieving objectives, 8–10
Activeness, on LinkedIn, 35–36
Activity generation, 101–102
Advocates, 28–29
Alumni, 26–27
Asking for introductions, xi, 45–72
  about, 45–48
  after you've asked, 57–59
  commitments, getting, 57–59
  delivery, 51–52
  feedback, 71–72
  framing, 49–51
  how to ask, 52–57
  phrases to avoid, 53–54
  scripts, 64–71
  specificity of, 54–57
  staging, 49–51
  what-ifs, preparing for, 59–64
  when to ask, 48–52
Attention, of referrals, 99–100
Attitude:
  attitude questions, for referrals, 110–111
  importance of in impression preparation, 76–78
  positive, 150
Attorneys, 25
Auerbach, Red, 13
Authenticity, on Facebook, 38

B

Beginning questions, for referrals, 109–110
Benefits, talking about, 114–118
Bloomberg, as source of information, 85

Branding, as responsibility of coaches, 190
Brethren, 29–30
Buddies, 29–30
Building essential partner network, xi, 23–44
  about, 23–24
  advocates, 28–29
  brethren/buddies, 29–30
  casual contacts, 30
  contact forms, 42–44
  contact lists, creating, 24–27
  diamonds in the rough, 31–32
  lists, organizing, 39–42
  people, categorizing, 27–28
  social media, 32–39
Buying signals, 118–119

C

Candor, as criteria for coach, 187
Casual acquaintances, 26
Casual contacts, 30
Categorizing people, 27–28
Centers of influence as referrals, xi, 123–143
  about, 123–125
  first meeting, 130–132
  meeting, 137–141
  meetings, calling for, 127–130
  numbers of, narrowing, 135
  opportunity, developing, 132–133
  pivoting, 133–135
  potential, 125–127
  referral lead exchange, calling for, 136–137
  tracking mechanism, 141–143
Chamber of commerce, 88
Citing history, 152–153
Client acquisition activities:
  asking for introductions, xi, 45–72

Client acquisition activities (*Cont.*):
  building essential partner network,
    xi, 23–44
  efficiency and effectiveness
    improvement, xi, 167–192
  impression preparation, xi, 73–91
  objective setting and strategy
    preparation, xi, 1–21
  referrals:
    centers of influence as, xi,
      123–143
    creating long-term network, xi,
      211–217
    speaking with, xi, 93–122
    thriving in changing times, xi,
      145–165
  what-ifs, xi, 193–209
Clients:
  colleagues of, 205–206
  contacting, 125–126
  current, 25
  educating, 153–154
  former, 25
  management, as responsibility of
    coaches, 189
  prospective, 25
  retention, as responsibility of
    coaches, 189
  scripts for voicemail for, 198
  target, 3–6
  "wallet-share" from existing, 206
Close friends, 26
Closing, 119–122
Coaches:
  expectations of, 191–192
  reporting to, 185–192
  roles and responsibilities, 187–192
  selecting, 186–187
COIs (*see* Centers of influence as
    referrals)
Colleagues of clients, 205–206
Commitment questions, for referrals,
    111–113
Commitments:
  getting, 57–59
  getting from referrals, 108,
    118–122
  signals, 118–119

Communication:
  about, 149
  being proactive, 152
  being there for your clients,
    155–156
  with clients, 125–126
  confidence, displaying, 149–150
  educating, 153–154
  e-mail, 202
  history, citing, 152–153
  ideas, providing new, 155
  leadership, demonstrating,
    151–152
  positive attitude, 150
Confidence, displaying, 149–150
Consistency, on Facebook, 38
Contact forms, 42–44
Contact lists, creating, 24–27
Contacts:
  neighbors and friends of,
    204–205
  scripts for voice mail for, 198
Coworkers, as source of information,
    82–83
CPAs, 25, 90–91
Critical success factors, 16–18
Current clients, 25
Current coworkers, as source of
    information, 82–83

D
Delayed introductions, 203–204
Delivery, of requests for introductions,
    51–52
Demonstrating leadership, 151–152
Developing opportunities with
    centers of influence, 132–133
Diamonds in the rough, 31–32
Directness, on LinkedIn, 35
Discounted dollar value, 179
Due diligence preparation questions,
    89–91

E
Educating clients, 153–154
Effectiveness improvement (*see*
    Efficiency and effectiveness
    improvement)

Efficiency and effectiveness
improvement, xi, 167–192
about, 167–168
coach roles and responsibilities,
187–192
coaches, reporting to, 185–192
expectations, exceeding, 185–192
pipeline management, 172–180
time management, 180–185
timeline for plan, 168–171
El-Erain, Mohamed, 153
E-mail communications, 202
Essential partners, 25–26
Even keel, 164
Exceeding expectations, 185–192
Executing plans, 19–20
Expectations, exceeding, 185–192
Experience, as criteria for coach,
187

F
Facebook, 37–39, 85
Family, 26
Family offices, due diligence
preparation questions on,
90–91
Features, talking about, 114–118
Feedback, giving yourself, 71–72
Fields, in lists, 40–42
50 percent scenario, 178
Focus:
on LinkedIn, 35
of objectives, 6
Former clients, 25
Former coworkers, as source of
information, 82–83
Framing requests for introductions,
49–51
Friends:
close, 26
of contacts, 204–205

G
Gatekeepers, 199–202
Giving and receiving, 214–217
Google, as source of information, 84
Growth, as selling cue, 163
Grunfeld, Joe, 215–216

H
Harmon, Butch, 185–186
History, citing, 152–153
Honesty:
as criteria for coach, 187
on LinkedIn, 35
Hoovers, as source of information,
85
How to ask for introductions, 52–57

I
Ideas, providing new, 155
Impression preparation, xi, 73–91
about, 73–76
attitude, 76–78
due diligence preparation questions,
89–91
identifying what you need to know,
78–80
sources of information, 80–89
Individuals, due diligence preparation
questions on, 89–91
Information gathering, from referrals,
107–113
Information giving, to referrals, 107–
108, 113–118
Internet, as source of information,
84–85
Introductions, delayed, 203–204
(*See also* Asking for introductions)
Involvement, on LinkedIn, 35

J
Jordan, Michael, 77

K
Koch, Ed, 16

L
Law firms, due diligence preparation
questions on, 90–91
Leadership, demonstrating, 151–152
LinkedIn, 33–37, 84
Listening, as responsibility of coaches,
190–191
Lists:
creating, 125
organizing, 39–42

Lose-lose relationship, 159–160
Lose-win relationship, 157–159

M

Management (client), as responsibility
    of coaches, 189
Marketing, as responsibility of
    coaches, 190
McCann, Bob, 148
Meetings:
    with centers of influence, 130–132,
        137–141
    with coaches, 191
    with referrals, 107–122
Mickelson, Phil, 185–186

N

Narrowing number of COI
    relationships, 135
Neighbors of contacts, 204–205
Network building, xi, 23–44
    about, 23–24
    advocates, 28–29
    brethren/buddies, 29–30
    casual contacts, 30
    contact forms, 42–44
    contact lists, creating, 24–27
    diamonds in the rough, 31–32
    lists, organizing, 39–42
    people, categorizing, 27–28
    social media, 32–39
Network creation from referrals, xi,
    211–217
    about, 211–213
    giving and receiving, 214–217
    networking, 213–214
90 percent scenario, 178

O

Objections to asking for
    introductions, 61–64
Objective setting and strategy
    preparation, xi, 1–21
    about, 3, 8
    accountability, 13–15
    characteristics of objectives, 6–8

importance of, 1–2
plans, executing, 19–20
plans, streamlining, 11–13
quantifiable metrics, 15–18
Summary Form, 21
supporting strategies, developing,
    8–13
target clients, 3–6
ways to achieve objectives, 8–10
Objectivity, as criteria for coach, 187
O'Neill, Paul, 168
Optimization, as responsibility of
    coaches, 189
Organizing lists, 39–42
Overconfident, 164–165

P

Partners, essential, 25–26
    (*See also* Building essential partner
        network)
People, categorizing, 27–28
Percent of closure, 178–179
Persuasiveness, on LinkedIn, 35
Phrases to avoid, when asking for
    introductions, 53–54
Pipeline management, 172–180
Pitch, 207–209
Pivoting, 133–135
Planning strategies (*see* Objective
    setting and strategy preparation)
Positioning statement, 100–101
Positive attitude, 150
Post-call debriefing, 106–107
Posting articles on LinkedIn, 36–37
Pre-call advice, 95–96
Proactive, being, 152
Professional contacts, 26
Professionalism, on LinkedIn, 34–35
Proof sources, talking about, 114–118
Prospective clients, 25
Pruning business, 156–160

Q

Quantifiable metrics, in objective
    setting and strategy preparation,
    15–18

R

Reactions, triggering, 101–102
Receiving and giving, 214–217
Recognizability, on Facebook, 38
Referral network sustainable process,
    15–16
Referrals:
    attention of, 99–100
    centers of influence as, xi, 123–143
        about, 123–125
        first meeting, 130–132
        meeting, 137–141
        meetings, calling for, 127–130
        numbers of, narrowing, 135
        opportunity, developing,
            132–133
        pivoting, 133–135
        potential, 125–127
        referral lead exchange, calling for,
            136–137
        tracking mechanism, 141–143
    creating long-term network, xi,
        211–217
        about, 211–213
        giving and receiving, 214–217
        networking, 213–214
    meeting with, 107–122
    person who gives you, 81–82
    scripts for voice mail for, 198–199
    speaking with, xi, 93–122
        about, 93–95
        commitments, getting,
            118–122
        features, benefits, and proof
            sources, 114–118
        for first time, 99–102
        information gathering, 107–113
        information giving, 107–108,
            110–111, 113–118
        meeting, preparing for, 107–122
        needs of, 109
        post-call, 106–107
        pre-call advice, 95–96
        scripts, 102–106
        types of questions, 109–113
        what-ifs, 96–99

Registry of Nonprofits, 88
Reliability, as criteria for coach, 187
Reporting to coaches, 185–192
Retention (client), as responsibility of
    coaches, 189
Rodriguez, Alex, 191
ROI (return on investment), 16
Role playing, as responsibility of
    coaches, 190

S

Sales & Marketing Management
    (magazine), 119
Salmon Scale of Sensibility, 176–180
Sample Contact Form, 44
Scripting, as responsibility of coaches,
    190
Scripts:
    for asking for introductions,
        64–71
    for clients' voice mail, 198
    for contacts' voice mail, 198
    for referrals' voice mail, 198–199
    for speaking with referrals,
        102–106
Search.com, as source of information,
    84–85
Second-degree connections
    (LinkedIn), 34
Selling cues, 160–165
Setting expectations, for requests for
    introductions, 49–51
Setting objectives (*see* Objective
    setting and strategy preparation)
75 percent scenario, 178
Sharma, Raj, 186
Social media, 32–39
    about, 32–33
    Facebook, 37–39, 84
    LinkedIn, 33–37, 84
    Twitter, 39
Sources of information, for
    impression preparation, 80–89
Speaking with referrals, xi, 93–122
    about, 93–95
    commitments, getting, 118–122

Speaking with referrals (*Cont.*):
  features, benefits, and proof sources, 114–118
  for first time, 99–102
  information gathering, 108–109
  information giving, 110–111
  meeting, preparing for, 107–122
  needs of, 109
  post-call, 106–107
  pre-call advice, 95–96
  scripts, 102–106
  types of questions, 109–113
  what-ifs, 96–99
Specificity, when asking for introductions, 54–57
Staging requests for introductions, 49–51
Standards of performance, 16–18
Strategies (*see* Objective setting and strategy preparation)
Strategizing, as responsibility of coaches, 189–190
Streamlining plans, 11–13
Summary Form, objective setting and strategy preparation, 21
Syms, 154

T
Target clients, 3–6
10 percent scenario, 178
Thriving in changing times, xi, 145–165
  about, 145–146
  being proactive, 152
  being there for your clients, 155–156
  communication, 149–156
  confidence, displaying, 149–150
  educating, 153–154
  history, citing, 152–153
  ideas, providing new, 155
  leadership, demonstrating, 151–152
  positive attitude, 150
  pruning, 156–160
  selling cues, 160–165
  volatility, 146–149

Time management, 180–185
Timelines, for planning, 13–15
Tracking mechanism for COIs, 141–143
Trouble, as selling cue, 163
Trust, as criteria for coach, 188
25 percent scenario, 178
Twitter, 39

V
Volatility, 146–149

W
"Wallet-share" from existing clients, 206
Websites:
  of competitors as source of information, 86–87
  of organizations as source of information, 85–86
What you need to know, for impression preparation, 78–80
What-ifs, xi, 193–209
  about, 193–194
  colleagues of clients, 205–206
  of contact or client conversations, 59–64
  delayed introductions, 203–204
  e-mail communications, 202
  gatekeepers, 199–202
  neighbors and friends of contacts, 204–205
  pitch, 207–209
  social friends as clients, 194–197
  voice mail, 197–199
  "wallet-share" from existing clients, 206
  when speaking with referrals, 96–99
When to ask for introductions, 48–52
Win-lose relationship, 157
Winning the business (*see* Client acquisition activities)
Win-win relationship, 156–157
Wooden, John, 2

About the Author

MICHAEL SALMON has been in the service business his entire professional life. He has helped countless people find what they want by showing them how to optimize their network of contacts. He holds the most valuable sort of PhD: Passionate, Hardworking, and Disciplined.

Salmon is the founder and CEO of Salmon Academy, Inc., one of the nation's foremost training, coaching, and sales consulting firms. His breakthrough concept of *Super-Networking*, the business application of "six degrees of separation," transforms networking from something vague and arbitrary into a sustainable process that leads to tangible results. Salmon developed his SuperNetworking methodology over the course of his three decades of leadership in improving sales, marketing, and management processes for both publicly traded and privately held companies.

Some of his clients include Merrill Lynch PBIG and GWM, Morgan Stanley Smith Barney, Sun Trust, UBS, Wells Fargo Advisors, Bank of America, Fiduciary Trust, Credit Suisse, HSBC, PIMCO, BlackRock, Lincoln Financial, Hewlett-Packard, Oracle, Deloitte, Boeing, United Technologies, VIACOM, AON, Milliman, and Harvard Business School. Salmon currently coaches several Fortune 500 executives and more than 40 of the Barron's and Worth's top 1,000 financial advisors. He has won recognition as an expert on the subjects of networking, sales, coaching, and consulting. Salmon was a keynote speaker at the last COMDEX, between Bill Gates and Scott McNealy.

He was also a panelist at SkyBridge Capital's 2011 SALT Conference, talking about successful marketing and sales strategies. A much sought-after speaker, he has explained the amazing power of SuperNetworking on FNC *Fox & Friends*, CNN, Bloomberg, NBC *Weekend Today in New York*, and CBS *Weekend Morning Show*. His comments often appear in such national publications as *USA Today, Investor's Business Daily, L.A. Times, Chicago Tribune, New York Newsday*, and *Entrepreneur* magazine. He has authored two other books, *SuperNetworking for Sales Pros* (Career Press, 2005), and *SuperNetworking: Access the Right People, Build Your Career Network, and Land Your Dream Job—Now!* (Career Press, 2003).

Salmon started his career at Pinkerton's, where he turned in top sales performances year after year. He also served as director of sales and marketing for UGL Unicco. He later became the VP of sales and marketing at First Security. Salmon often worked with placement firms when staffing his own departments and saw how the best in the industry conducted business. He combined those best practices with the blue chip service delivery model developed over his many years in business when he ultimately founded his own company, Berkshire Staffing. Some of Salmon's clients were Liberty Mutual, Hewlett-Packard, State Street Bank, Goldman Sachs, and JPMorgan Chase.

After Salmon sold Berkshire to a major national staffing organization, he decided to focus exclusively on teaching the networking program he had perfected over time. Salmon graduated with a B.S from Northeastern University.